Reconstructing Shakespeare

Rebuilding His Plays in Contemporary Literary Environment

Reconstructing Shakespeare

Rebuilding His Plays in Contemporary Literary Environment

Edited by

V Lakshmanan

AUTHORSPRESS
Publishers of Scholarly Books

Worldwide Circulation through Authorspress Global Network
First Published 2011
by
Authorspress
E-35/103, Jawahar Park
Laxmi Nagar, Delhi-110 092
e-mail: authorspress@yahoo.com

Reconstructing Shakespeare:
Rebuilding His Plays in Contemporary Literary Environment
ISBN 978-81-7273-563-0

Printed in India at Tarun Offset, Delhi.

Preface

This book is a collection of papers presented at the seminar on *Reconstructing Shakespeare: Rebuilding His Plays in Contemporary Literary Environment* (2-3 March 2009) organized by me at the Department of English, Annamalai University with support from University Grants Commission. Reinterpreting Shakespeare in the framework of contemporary critical theories was the thrust area of the seminar. Indeterminacy or shifting of meaning is fundamental to contemporary literary theories. Deconstruction has caused revaluation and reinterpretation of old literary texts. Elaine Showalter became actively involved with feminism only during the time when she re-evaluated the novels of Bronte to Lessing in her treatise *A Literature of Their Own* (1977). Similarly, with the accepted ideas of Edward Said in "Orientalism," Shakespeare's *The Tempest* began to be viewed on the post-colonial binaries of sameness/otherness. Gender critics began to hypothesize that there is something maimed about the concentration of the men characters and the exclusively masculine world of Rome in *Antony and Cleopatra*; the alternative, they thought, is figured in Cleopatra in Egypt who swallows up the public sphere in her personal experience. More and more of Shakespearean plays were finding such newer and newer interpretations. Our teachers and students of literature invariably needed updating of their knowledge of the great bard. Realizing this need, the present seminar was organized. The prime purpose of the seminar was to swap knowledge: to interpret Shakespeare through modern critical theories and comprehend modern critical theories through Shakespeare. In effect, the seminar was a trailblazer attempt to resurrect, for example, Macbeth from his grave with Derrida's powerful magic wand.

The three highlights of the seminar were: first and foremost the seminar was student-friendly; our students might have already known the story-line of one or many plays of Shakespeare and this awareness in them was exploited to introduce them to new critical theories. Second, through the papers read in the seminar, the students became consciously aware that a text can have more than one meaning, which in literary phrasing, is called plurality or multiplicity of meaning. Third, at a time when literatures throughout the world were getting pigeonholed because of their provincial and parochial outlook, a re-valuation of classics like Shakespeare was felt to be necessary.

The seminar was spread over four plenaries and nine paper reading sessions. A total of 72 papers were read. Twenty-one of them are collected in this volume. The articles collected here represent a wide range of topics covered, from the purely theoretical—psychoanalytical approach to Shakespeare including Freudian theories, Jung and the theory of archetypes, cultural materialism, gender studies including political feminism, boy actors, queer theory and transvestism, postcolonial criticism, political Shakespeare, intertextuality, Shakespeare in performance and Shakespeare in the classroom—to the thematically specific, such as Hamlet's insanity, Hamlet as a man of tradition and redefining Macbeth.

The volume begins with Professor Chellappan's article, "Reconstructing Shakespeare: The World as Theatre," in which he has emphasised the universality and timelessness of Shakespeare and has stated that each age has rediscovered Shakespeare in its own image and in that process rediscovered itself. Today, feminists, new historicists, Marxists and post-colonial critics have brought new perspectives to make Shakespeare relevant to the chaos of contemporary life and respond to new critical theories. The focus of Professor Chellappan's article is Shakespeare's treatment of power as "theatre." Analysing *King Lear, Hamlet* and *Twelfth Night,* based on critical insights from Stephen Greenblatt, Jonathan Dollimore and Janet Adelman, the author confirms that though they vary in several aspects, all of them are concerned with the prospects of power.

Evolution and shaping of public spaces is an area of contemporary interest in literary studies. B. Hariharan in his article "The Dynamics of Public Spaces in Shakespeare" locates his discovery of public spaces in some of Shakespeare's plays against a historical framework, from the perspective of the interpretive freedom that one can bring in while producing the plays and also how much the playwright was aware of the place available for his craft.

Baniprata Goswami disputes the power-magic relationship in *The Tempest* in his article "Power of Magic and Magic of Power." Even though its romance ethos cannot be denied, Baniprata remarks, the play has the distinct political theme of power and legitimacy. This postcolonial interpretation of the play is further complicated with the issue of magic, which in spite of its art and cultural identity, is conventionally the natural associate of romance. But in the play, magic, itself a construct of power, has been exploited to capture and ensure political and cultural authority. The author connects this to the present day world politics, especially on the issue of globalization, and confirms the significance of this political deception, adopted and employed four hundred years ago.

Raju Parghi in "Power, Dominance, and Survival in Shakespeare's Last Plays" looks at these plays in terms of politics of power, dominance, and survival placing *The Tempest* at the centre. The practice of interpreting *The Tempest* from postcolonial perspectives, as in the case of the previous article, has paved the way for the other three plays to be looked into focusing on the struggle for and sustaining of power. Parghi argues that Pericles's struggles to reunite with his daughter in *Pericles*, Cymbeline's reluctance to marry his daughter to Posthumus in *Cymbeline*, and Leontes's suspicion of his wife Hermione in *The Winter's Tale* are all actions highlighting the archetypal human nature for domination and thrust for survival.

Edward Bond's *Bingo* is a revisionist reading of Shakespeare's world and works. Bond being a Marxist writer foregrounds the social responsibility of a writer. He believes that social corrections can be done through theatres. In this regard, the relationship between the writer and the society problematizes the whole concept of writing and reading. Harini Jayaraman and K. Sreena in "Shakespeare: A Capitalist?" attempt to read Bond's *Bingo* in the Marxist critical perspective and also to interrogate the inequity in Shakespeare: the materialistic bent of mind in the 'real' Shakespeare disintegrates him as an artist. The main thrust of Bond's criticism of Shakespeare is that he never tried to explore the realities of his time, but solely depended on the historical facts.

With the onset of globalization and free market, literature, especially classical literature, is being pushed to a backseat in the modern consciousness. Nevertheless, that does not mean Shakespeare is losing his relevance. Such brilliance as that of Shakespeare cannot be wiped out by the trivialities of passing trends. However, it has become imperative now, more than ever, that we rediscover Shakespeare and fit him into the present day mould. Punyashree Panda in "Living through Future: Shakespeare in the Management Classroom" looks into such interesting possibilities and the implications thereof. Her article seeks to establish Shakespeare as a modern day communicator in whose writing there are lessons abound for the future managers of this country. This article also suggests some stimulating and practicable ideas to customise Shakespeare in the modern classroom environment and make Shakespeare and the ambience livelier.

The postmodern era is one in which replacement takes over from the original. For Marxist critics like Terry Eagleton and Fredric Jameson and French theorist Jean Baudrillard, postmodern culture is dominated by the simulacrum or the copy, which has come to replace the "real." In the tradition of these theories and practices, Aysha Viswamohan in "Scottish Highlands to Feudal Japan: *Macbeth* and *The Throne of Blood*" looks at the two creations primarily as social tragedies set within a distanced historical context. *The Throne of Blood* is a rich text that benefits from a viewing that includes knowledge of *Macbeth,* as much as it is enriched by familiarity with Japanese culture. It is new and yet timeless, largely due to the fusion of its two main sources and cultures: Shakespeare's English play and Japanese Noh theatre.

The "Garrison theatre" patronized by British colonists gets the credit of performing the first Shakespearean plays in India. From then on till today, there have been many plays in original, adaptations, translations in many Indian languages, and also cinematic adaptations. Asha Priya and Priya in "Imprint of Shakespeare on the Indian Stage and Screen" state that localizing

Shakespeare had never been a problem. Playpen, a theatre group managed by Mahesh Dattani, put up a cross-cultural presentation of *The Tempest* where Prospero wears dhoti and the other characters look as if they have just come out of the Indian folk theatre. On another occasion, an adapted version of *Othello* in Kathakali form was staged. It was enacted in the very traditional manner in front of the flickering flames of a brass lamp, with the typical *thirasheela* (curtain) used for dramatic effects. Ania Loomba calls the Kathakali version of *Othello* an example of post-colonial hybrid Shakespeare. The advent of such hybrid Shakespeare "provincialized Shakespeare" and the present day Indian local dramatics makes Shakespeare's plays very much relevant.

Shruti Bidwaikar in "The Force in Shakespeare's plays: in Sri Aurobindo's Perspective" tells us that Sri Aurobindo does not necessarily formulate a theory on Shakespeare's plays, but reveals the element which has sustained its popularity and affectivity. This element is the play of life-force, the vital impulse. She reiterates, with fairly lengthy quotations from *Macbeth,* that Shakespeare's plays do not merely portray men in action but, show men governed by life-forces, by their passions, ambitions, feelings and hatred.

The African American writer Gloria Naylor's novels are linked by a set of internal cross-references to characters and places in Shakespeare's works. Naylor's involvement and negotiations with Shakespeare occur in an intermediate zone that conveys a delicate tension in Naylor's perspective on Shakespeare. Deivasigamani in "Shakespeare's Voice in Gloria Naylor's *Mama Day*" showcases the inter-textual allusion of Naylor's mythical love story *Mama Day* to *The Tempest*. Both Shakespeare and Naylor are different in race, gender, time and space; but the fundamental tension in life is to connect the mysterious voices within ourselves – voices too often muffled by the roar of social conventions, regionalism, racism and sexism.

Geetha Senthilkumar, Ambika and Krishnalalitha in "Masculine Traits in the Feminine Self" have studied Shakespeare's plays based on Jungian theory, bringing out the unique reality of their gender construction. The authors have analysed the *animus* (the masculine trait) in the three main female characters of Shakespeare, Portia in *The Merchant of Venice,* Lady

Macbeth in *Macbeth* and Rosalind in *As You Like It*. Gendered disguise in *The Merchant of Venice* and *As You Like It* empowers Portia and Rosalind; disguise not only provides these characters with visual masculinity, but imbues them with a stronger voice and sense of dramatic self. But, Lady Macbeth openly attempts to reject her feminine traits and adopt a male posture because she perceives that her society associates feminine qualities with weakness. She is convinced that she must divest herself of her femininity if she needs to influence her husband's public life. N. Chandra's "Masculinity and Disguise: A Study of Portia and Viola" is an extension of the above article. Chandra affirms that only in disguise, Portia and Viola are accepted and acknowledged for their "bravery", "intelligence" and "manliness."

Smitha in her article, "ShakesQueer: A Queer Reading of Shakespeare," has raised and answered questions like Was Hamlet a gay? Why is Othello separated from Desdemona? Who are the queer virgin characters in Shakespeare's plays? Was Shakespeare himself a gay? She has also discussed the queer influence on John Madden's Oscar winning movie, *Shakespeare in Love.* Studies done by queer theorists have redefined Shakespeare. Some of the queer theorists endeavoured on analyzing the coding of Shakespeare where they found many underlying and shocking references to gay and lesbian relationships. Such revelations on the mystery of Shakespeare received much more attention with the implications of post-structuralism and deconstruction. His works, the queer theorists said, should be considered as symbolic constructs of a thing signified. Many of his comedies, tragedies and sonnets are now re-read to discover new meanings which are linked to queer ideology.

Another gender related concept is transvestism. Subhapriya in "Transvestism in Shakespeare's *As You Like It*" has described the dramatic practice of transvestism in a range of cultures by comparing Shakesperare's *As You Like It* with the Kabulki *Onnagata* and the Peking Opera *Dans.* Transvestism has been an essential part of dramatic performances for a long time—differently in different cultures. Each culture had resorted to transvestism in its theatre as a result of forbidding women on the stage.

Parimala's "Othello: A Study of the 'Self' and the 'Other'" is a winding back to the notion of postcolonial power structures which we discussed in two of the earlier articles with reference to *The Tempest* and other last plays. The paper attempts to explore the internal working of the colonial mind by analyzing the major characters Iago and Othello.

Sangeetha in "Katharina Wronged" reads *The Taming of the Shrew* in a gynocentric perspective. Shakespeare's women characters are invariably powerful, pleasant, intelligent, tactful and courageous. Why Katharina alone is portrayed as a shrew? Did Shakespeare want to show her differently or was he too a male chauvinist? Or does Katharina mellow down due to her real love for her husband? Or is she having the last laugh with her subdued speech towards the end? Sangeetha analyses the play from these aspects.

In "Redefining *Macbeth*," Santhosh Kumar makes a wicked but valid revelation that it is not out of ambition but because of love that Macbeth kills Duncan. If Duncan, a weakling in his dotage, had not died, he would have lived an ignoble life. Macbeth, who has been serving as a faithful lieutenant continues to do so by bringing death to Duncan as death is that unconquerable liberating force which helps man to reach the undisturbed state. Since the argument sounds illogical, strong theories and evidences are stated in support.

The problem of problems in *Hamlet* is Hamlet's insanity. Ravichandran's article "Hamlet's Insanity as Defence Mechanism" subscribes to the view that Hamlet is not really mad but feigns madness. At one stage in the play, when Hamlet becomes aware that he has no access to pursue his ideal and dream, all the glory and the brilliance once he possessed vanishes all of a sudden into the air. The people around him turn to be ignoble and inhuman, and there is no room for reality therefore his life turns out tedious. He wavers in the conflict between the ideal and reality, on the brink of the question—"To be or not to be." He chooses to feign madness which is a need as well as a defence mechanism for him to struggle against reality. Life teases him and his madness teases his rivals.

Colette Sharmila in "Anti-Semitism in *The Merchant of Venice*" upholds Shylock and his creator Shakespeare. The Jew was a figure hated by Elizabethans; the Elizabethans also hated the traditional Jewish profession of usury. Shylock is two-times ill-fated, he is a Jew, and he is a money-lender. Shylock, the money-lender who is hated because he is a Jew, explains how prejudice works. He calls prejudice as the master emotion which directs our emotion to love or hate the objects of our prejudice. Jews were often forbidden to own land or to engage in trade in England; as a result the only profession open to them was money-lending. Shylock's wealth is evidence of his professional success. One can think of shylock as a "real" person, whose words and deeds are provoked by Christian thoughts and actions.

Suresh Frederick in "Pericles and the Sea" makes an archetypal reading of Shakespeare's *Pericles.* Frederick thinks of the sea as an archetype in which background the play's action takes place. Throughout the play, the sea, because of its immense power and fury, encompasses "the tragic vision." But it makes amends for the damage done. Even though Pericles calls it the "watery grave" it takes him safely to the shore in spite of the raging tempest which leaves him bereft of all his fortunes.

Obviously, all the papers in this collection through the seminar theme of "Reconstructing Shakespeare" seek to address the shared knowledge and experience of two rich and different studies—Shakespeare and literary criticism. These aspects—as they relate Shakespeare to archetypal, psychological, philosophical, postcolonial and gender studies and such other categories—unify the papers in this volume.

It is hoped that this book will be of interest and use to the general readers and students and scholars of literature who are sure to find something new and challenging in this ever-evolving discussion.

26 June 2010 ***V. Lakshmanan***

Acknowledgements

I wish to gratefully acknowledge the authorities of Annamalai University and my colleagues at the Department of English for help and general support.

I thank all the contributors to this book of collection of essays on Shakespeare.

I thank Liliana Osses Adams for allowing me to use the image for cover design from her copyrighted materials.

I wish to record my appreciation and thankfulness to my friend and publisher, Sudarshan Kcherry, Authorspress, for making this collection available to readers.

Above all, with all humility, I thank God for all His goodness.

V. Lakshmanan

Contents

1

Reconstructing Shakespeare: The World as Theatre

— K. Chellappan

Ben Jonson's remark that Shakespeare is "not of an age, but for all time" sums up the universality and timelessness of Shakespeare. Each age has rediscovered Shakespeare in its own image and in that process rediscovered itself. The eighteenth century saw in his plays a mirror held up to nature; the nineteenth century romanticized him and found in his plays the portrayal of the infinity of human mystery. In A.C. Bradley, we see the culmination of psychological criticism and a Hegelian interpretation of Shakespearean tragedy. The first part of the twentieth century gave importance to his poetry and imagery as well as its theatrical elements. There were also attempts to give a Christian interpretation to his plays.

But in the second part of the twentieth century feminists, new historicists, Marxists and post-colonial/modern critics have brought new perspectives to make Shakespeare relevant to the chaos of contemporary life and respond to new critical theories. Though they vary in several aspects, all of them are concerned with the theme of power in Shakespeare's plays. The focus of this paper is Shakespeare's treatment of power as "theatre."

Most feminists focus on the female body or the way the gender influences language and try to show how Shakespeare's women differ from men because they are able to develop an identity in harmony with their mothers, unlike men who suffer from fear of an engulfing mother. This is based on object relations theory. Janet Adelman refers to the absence of mother in *King Lear* and talks of the presence of the figure of the suffocating mother from *Hamlet* onwards. She has also suggested that strong women were often perceived, represented and repressed as a source of threat.

In comedies women are portrayed more positively and even aggressively and for this purpose Shakespeare's use of disguise gives women freedom and power but only temporarily. Though Rosalind, Viola and Portia acquire full identity through the male garb, there is something sad and incomplete in their final acceptance of femininity, and the plays seem to achieve no solutions but only artistic resolutions, and the sense of an ending which is a necessity of the masculine imagination. In the words of Marina Warner:

> Historically, transvestism has often provided a device for a woman to make something of herself, a figure of speech to lay claim to greatness beyond the potential of her sex. Like many devices, it is practical and yet mysterious, convenient and yet magic, all at once, and its provoking, fascinating quality has made it a motif in tragedy, folklore, mythology, hagiography, ritual, romance and children's stories. (13)

Shakespearean heroines also use disguise which liberates their true self. To take the most prominent examples, Rosalind's resort to disguise is compelled by a set of sudden circumstances which force her to search for a new identity in the Forest of Arden which gives her freedom from social restraints as well as the limitations of her sex. She enjoys new found liberation but also the power which the persona brings—she objectifies her animus with which she comes to terms and thereby with Orlando. Her double consciousness of the self-and-the-mask or the self-as-the-mask beautifully plays with the consciousness of the audience who are more aware of the situation than she herself is. But there is a conflict between the masculine appearance and the feminine sensibility. She is conscious of this disparity right from the beginning:

> We'll have a swashing and a martial outside,
> As many other mannish cowards have
> That do outface it with their semblances. (1. 3. 116–8)

Again she says,

> Dost thou think, though I am
> Caparisoned like a man, I have a doublet
> And hose in my disposition? (3. 2. 178–9)

Critics like Madelon Sprengnether feel that both the Anglo-American and the Lacanian versions of Freud only sustain the gender hierarchy because what the two psychoanalytic traditions reveal is that "femininity in the unconscious order of patriarchy signifies subversion." From this point of view,

> the male actor in female dress represents femininity as masquerade on the one hand, as a role that can be appropriated by a man in his relations with other men; on the other hand, he seems to call into question the traditional hierarchy of male or female along with a possibility of a secure sexual identity. The conflicting attributes towards femininity separately articulated in contemporary psychoanalytic theory find expression here in a single figure. The convention of stage transvestism makes explicit the interdependence of these seemingly contradictory positions. The convention of cross-dressing itself may be viewed as a symptomatic expression of the patriarchal construction of femininity. It speaks to an anxiety about masculine identity based on the representation of woman as 'other' at the same time that it seems to allay that anxiety by offering an image of an all male society. (7)

New historicists also discuss cross dressing in Shakespeare. Stephen Greenblatt in his article "Fiction and Friction" sees a link between the Elizabethan medical discourse which suggested the possibility of sexual transformation and Shakespeare's use of transvestism as there was circulation of power through discourses. Greenblatt states:

> We are dealing rather with a shared code, a set of interlocking tropes and similitudes that function not only as the objects but as the conditions of representation. Shakespearean comedy constantly appeals to the body in particular to sexuality as the heart of the theatrical magic; 'great creating nature' the principle by which the world is and must be peopled is the comic playwright's tutelary spirit. But there is no unmediated access to the body, no direct appropriation of sexuality; rather sexuality is itself a network of historically contingent figures that constitute the culture's categorical understanding of erotic experience. These figures function as modes of translation between distinct social discourses, channels through which cultural power is circulated. (*Shakespearean Negotiations* 78)

Greenblatt shows how fiction enacts friction in plays like *As You Like It* and women make love freely in disguise. He also sees a link between history and fiction and shows in "Shakespeare and the Exorcists" how Shakespeare used the theatre image in *King Lear* for exorcism, just as Homett's book uses exorcism as a kind of theatre:

> Edgar does to Gloucester what the theatre usually does to the audience; he persuades his father to discount the evidence of his senses, and to accept a palpable fiction; though we [the audience] enjoy being brazenly lied to but we withhold from the theatre the simple assent that we grant to every day reality. (*Contemporary Literary criticism* 46)

Shakespeare combines theatrical and religious traditions. He appropriates the function of rituals which the official secular and religious institutions were abjuring. There is hence an emptying out of the official position and what was literal has become the sacred and the sacred was reversed to the secular in the theatre.

Marxists see the impact of the power structure as well as role of economics even in plays like *King Lear*. When Lear asks his daughters to quantify their love, it is said that he treats love as commodity that has exchange value. Jonathan Dollimore also shows that when Lear is on the heath, he is moved to pity when he first witnesses houseless poverty: "You houseless poverty I have taken too little care of this." Lear bitterly reproaches himself that he had ignored the suffering of his deprived subjects. The distracted use of the abstract "You houseless poverty" subtly suggests that Lear's disregard has been of a general rather than local poverty. Dollimore continues:

> *King Lear* suggests here a profound truth. Far from endorsing the idea that man can redeem himself in and through an access of pity, we might be moved to recognize that, on the contrary, in a world where pity is the prerequisite for compassionate action, where the king has to share the suffering of his subjects in order to 'care' the majority will remain poor, naked, wretched. (198)

He also says that however the play insists on the gulf which separates the privileged from the deprived by insisting on the fictiveness of the genre. And this is clinched by the exchange between poor Tom and Gloucester which reveals the woeful inadequacy of kindness and how unkindness is built into social conscience.

Though the play cannot be reduced to Christian or existential humanism, one cannot deny that it transcends the socio-economic problems. The play vindicates the triumph of love over death, though there is still uncertainty. Initially, Lear demanded love and could not get it. Later, while identifying himself with the un-accommodated man, he is reborn through love which comes unsought with Cordelia. In the beginning, Shakespeare shows through Cordelia that love is speechless and that it cannot be demonstrated; at the end, Shakespeare shows that love is deathless and needs nothing on return, not even visible evidence. But modern criticism shows the complex process through which this is attained.

In the beginning Lear dismissed reality as illusion and accepted illusion as reality. The whole play combines the power with the illusion of theatre and the world as theatre merges with theatre as world.

Critics like Christopher Calderwood have studied "meta-drama" in Shakespeare's plays. The present writer has also studied meta-drama in *Henry IV Part I*. Even in *King Lear* we can see meta-drama. The opening scene of the play emphasizes the theatricality of power. King Lear seems to be an actor in more than one sense. Whereas Goneril and Regan "play" the expected roles very well, Cordelia "acts" true to her deeper self and her action is in conflict with the action of Lear and her sisters. When Lear demands "love" in the theatrical sense, Cordelia's "nothing" nullifies such a relationship between love and thing. To Cordelia love is an unutterable truth and it is unconditional and not dependent on anything.

Lear's subsequent fall is as dramatic as the dismissal of Cordelia and his error of judgement is revealed when he is rejected by the elder daughters he had chosen. When Lear enters the emptiness of the heath, he seems to be closer to reality, whereas in the world of power he seems to have enjoyed only a theatrical illusion. The Fool has been revealing the folly of his wisdom and the emptiness of power. In the final phase, again we see drama within drama. When Cordelia is dead, he accepts illusion as reality and refuses to believe that Cordelia is dead. In the opening scene, he believed in the illusion of his power and the drama of his children, at the end, love negates the negation of death.

James Howe's *A Buddhist Shakespeare* comments on the deferral of identity in Prince Hal in *Henry IV Part I* and *Hamlet* with the Derridean deferral and the Buddhist denial of identity. Hal fulfils the role as a warrior but by giving away his honour to Falstaff; he too takes it as a play-thing like Falstaff.

Similarly, when Hamlet accepts the challenge to play in the final duel, the duel-play synthesis is complete. He is no longer imprisoned by or obsessed with the past and now there is a new acceptance of full presence, including its traces of past and future. From our point of view Hamlet is a soldier-player. Whereas, Fortinbras is all soldier and Horatio, a detached philosopher-player, Hamlet combines both. Probably, Krishna's advice to Arjuna in the battlefield also visualizes life as a playground-cum-battleground and we should act our roles as players even in the battlefield.

Though Shakespeare's last play *The Tempest* has been considered as a play on colonialism, Prospero as the colonizer and Caliban as the colonized, most critics agree on the importance of the theme of power. The magic of Prospero creates an illusion. The play sees the world as a dream, or a play, enacted by Prospero and we are told:

> We are such stuff
> As dreams are made on, and our little life
> Is rounded with a sleep. (4. 1. 157—9)

After manipulating several things, Prospero is led to break off the betrothal masque and say "Our revels now are ended." Stephen Greenblatt refers to his speech as the brooding meditation on the theatrical insubstantiality of the entire world and the dream-like nature of human experience. Theatre, to Shakespeare, was a metaphor and means of discovering the world—with all its unreal reality, but which is also the only "real" reality which we can hope to have. "Was it a vision or a dream?" This is a question Shakespeare has been asking all the time and all criticism has not answered it and the mystery of the world and Shakespeare are mysteries still.

Works Cited

Adelman, Janet. *Suffocating Mother's Fantasies: Maternal Origin of Shakespeare's Plays Hamlet to The Tempest.* New York: Routledge, 1992.

Calderwood, James L. *Metadrama in Shakespeare's Henriad: Richard II to Henry V.* Los Angeles: University of California Press, 1979.

Chellappan, K. "Metadrama in *Henry IV Part I.*" *Indian Journal of English Studies* (1981-2): 187-195.

Dollimore, Jonathan and Alan Sinfield. "King Lear." *Radical Tragedy: Religion, Ideology and Power in the Drama of Shakespeare and His Contemporaries.* Durham: Duke University, 1984: 189-202.

Greenblatt, Stephen. "Fiction and Friction." *Shakespearean Negotiations.* Los Angeles: Universsity of California Press, 1989.

_____________ . "Shakespeare and the Exorcists." *Contemporary Literary Criticism.* Eds. Robert Con Davis and Ronald Schaefer. London: Longman, 1988.

Howe, James. *A Buddhist's Shakespeare.* London: OUP, 1994.

Sprengnether, Madelon. "Feminism, Shakespeare, Psycho-analysis: An Introduction." Paper presented at World Shakespeare Congress, West Berlin, 1985.

Warner, Marina. '"Joan of Arc' in *As You Like It.*" Paper presented at Shakespeare Conference in Stratford upon Avon, 1985.

2

The Dynamics of Public Spaces in Shakespeare: A Preliminary Exploration

— B. Hariharan

> On this unworthy scaffold to bring forth
> So great an object: can this cockpit hold
> The vasty fields of France? or may we cram
> Within this wooden O the very casques
> That did affright the air at Agincourt?
>
> — *Henry V, Prologue*

Theatre and performance has always expressed public space, be it the ancient Greek, Roman, or Sanskrit theatre, or classical dance or folk performances like *Kutiyattam*. What sets apart classical theatre from performance is the use of the acting space as a continuation of the lived space of its audience. To give one instance, it is useful to remember the Dionysian festival in ancient Greece where plays were staged in competition which itself was a great theatre festival. Obviously, theatre has people gathering together like in a festival and it is possible to argue that the spatial formations on both instances is conditioned largely by different forms of human transaction that structures the dynamics of the event itself. Like during a festival, so too when a play is staged; another space is formed that brings together all ambivalences and contradictions in social relationships to exist in suspended time.

And yet, such an experience of space is built on a foundation that is essentially commercial. This paper is an attempt to describe such commercial space with particular reference to Shakespeare's scripts and stage and locate the dynamics of the ways in which the larger suburban and cultural geography found expression in the script as well as in the production on stage. I would also try to draw out the implications of this suburban and cultural geography to argue that Shakespeare's plays were more expressive of the space that kept the tills ringing rather than reduce it to a set of precepts that claim to echo an Aristotelian theory of art as imitation. To be very specific, it is important to recognize that when Dr. Johnson said that Shakespeare "holds a mirror up to life," ("Preface to Shakespeare") we seldom raise any doubt about the reference to "life" and straightaway read the comment as typical of eighteenth century English taste with a rich topping of the "moral" dimension that Johnson refers to while discussing the bard's tragedies.

Therefore, we have to turn to the location of the inns, playhouses and the amphitheatres on the Thames in the suburbs of London for "life" in Shakespeare's plays. Life that Shakespeare explored on stage definitely had a commercial dimension. For the playwright knew very well that the space where the words he penned would be uttered in action was largely commercial that had people who did rapid business. Shakespeare knew that he had to write for the marketplace. Rightly then, Bernard Beckerman observes that "Elizabethan theatre was one of the earliest examples of theatre as commercial enterprise" (2).

Though Beckerman makes this observation in the context of a study of the productions at the Globe during 1599-1609, it holds good for the economics that governed performances and availability of public spaces that were at once within and outside the rule of law. Plays were staged in private houses, public halls, and the inns with their yards converted into expressive theatres for such kinds of performances that were scripted even as the production was underway. For, the stage had a certain kind of freedom ascribed to the licentious nature of theatres. The business transactions that provided space for performance, the sale of gallery space for the spectator, food and accommodation for the players, and the sale of refreshments witnessed the production of another theatrical space that could illustrate such scripting.

Wai Fong Cheang discusses the importance of theatrical spaces in Shakespeare quoting Steven Mullaney when he comments upon the location of Renaissance theatres in the suburbs outside London city and its implications for the comedy in Shakespeare's history plays in particular. The location of the theatres outside the city of London, "allowed them to be places of licensed licentiousness where the dominant ideologies of the day could be played against the theatricality of the stage" ("Comic Spaces in Shakespeare's History Plays" 147).

One can read a much fascinating account of the public places that shaped the nature of Shakespearean plays in an essay by Stephen Greenblatt. Greenblatt provides a very useful context to locate the scenes, stage directions, and the dialogues in Shakespeare in the marketplace of ideas, "the wooden O." He calls the suburbs, "an all-purpose entertainment zone" as it harboured taverns, inns, "houses of resort" (brothels), firing ranges, cock-fighting pits, bowling alleys, places for music and dancing, bearbaiting rings, platforms for mutilating or hanging criminals, as well as theatres (Will in the World: How Shakespeare Became Shakespeare 176-81).

In other words, there was all round commercial activity and it is not right to say that only playgoers came for the productions. There could be non-playgoers who would come to the Globe or the Swan after finishing their business in "houses of resort"; people selling merchandise were regulars in the theatre. This borderland was the space that made Elizabethan England, thanks to the cultural life it generated outside of the city centre or the life in the court. The place would be bustling with people that set the tone for many of the bard's plays. The level of education and social standing therefore could be wide ranging, given particularly the cultural geography of the place. A very important point that emerges here about the city-space of London is that it was very puritan with its take on licentiousness and morality.

Before entering this cultural space, let me put one penny in the box that the admission collector (there are two of them) has in his hands. Both collectors will go to the room backstage—the box office—to keep the money before the play begins. I stand by the platform stage with the groundlings (stinkards in summer) to watch the play. Shakespeare wrote his plays for this stage which "project[s] halfway into the 'pit', also called the 'yard' (if tiled or cobbled)" (Michael Best: Online). I can see from here the "Gentleman's Room" or the "Lord's Room."

James G. McManaway says that the platform stage "is proving in use to be astonishingly flexible and enormously effective. And its employment, in pure or modified form, in several of the festivals and most of the off-Broadway productions, is one of the great factors in their success. It not only contributes to the enjoyment of the audiences but also discloses unnoted aspects of Shakespeare's mastery of stagecraft" (James G. McManaway viii).

The flexibility of such a stage gave Shakespeare the "freedom to present a rapid succession of scenes long or short, indoors or out, upstairs or down, or nowhere in particular. It was large enough to permit vigorous movement, crowds, spectacles, ceremonies; it was intimate enough to make it natural for an actor to pour out his soul in soliloquy or aside" (xii). The structure of the stage provided the playwright specific spaces that shaped the living dynamics of experiencing history, ideology, and politics, in the tangible moments of leisure. Leisure here is tangible because of the very structure of the theatre and the physical intimacy of the audience.

We get tc read the creation of one such space in a kind of historical and political understanding by the Queen herself in the context of the Essex rebellion after the staging of *Richard II*. This is an interesting case of a play at the Globe spatializing history as public discourse in the public figure of Essex leading the revolt. The stage in suburban London engaged Queen Elizabeth to appropriate imaginatively the spatial memory of the tragedy of Richard II in a remark she supposedly made, "'I am Richard II. Know ye not that?' The Queen's move to identity herself with Shakespeare's sympathetic Richard II manifests that the play had a potent political symbol and the Queen understood it. Moreover, it also suggests that the Queen perceived some kind of interconnection between the play and Essex's rebellion" (Wai Fong Cheang 152). Here we have one of those instances when the centre co-opts the suburban space to re-create a larger than life public figure that will be "present" every time the play is staged in those margins. In other words, the public space that the audience inhabited was immediately political and that is the larger context in which we may learn to read Shakespeare's history plays.

We may read spaces that Shakespeare writes into his plays in other ways. In *Henry IV Part I*, Shakespeare's art brings together

Prince Hal and Falstaff. "In *Henry IV,* the licentious tavern in Eastcheap, where Hal, Henry IV's prodigal son, hangs out with his indecent pal, Falstaff, is a site that encapsulates the spirit of the licentious Liberties in the Renaissance. It is a place of amusement with wine, whores and jestings. Moreover, it is a place for play acting," writes Wai Fong Cheang (153). Another way of understanding the coming together of the two men may be to keep in mind the special quality of suburban geography that inform the theatre. There are immediate identifiable markers here with which the audience could relate so much so that the inn-yard scene, tavern scenes, or jesting may be dramatic for the sheer spacing out on stage of the world outside.

For instance, consider the opening of Act 2 Scene 1 of *Henry IV Part I* in an inn-yard followed by the waylaying of the travellers. Such a scene may be one of those instances of a play within a play when we recall that plays were performed during winter in inn-yards even with the City Corporation regulating them. That is to say, people who are at the inn watch people coming to the inn in the play in an extended theatrical space. Even more fascinating is the location of the Boar's Head tavern in Eastcheap. The Bell Inn and Cross Keys were very near Eastcheap. The imagined tavern on stage would be a familiar, identifiable space and yet double as theatre outside the city-space for the adventures of the Prince and Falstaff. It is in such public spaces that we get to witness the upending of all authority with all its excesses to recognize the creation of this space of misrule with its subversive power.

From such English experience of spaces, it does not take much for Shakespeare to get to the streets elsewhere for other forms of spatial explorations. For instance, on stage, apart from the title *The Merchant of Venice* and the names of characters, what would help the audience imagine a street in Venice? Surely there were no sign boards on stage in Italian to indicate the city or language. In spite of the signs offered in the title to the streets in Venice, the audience only gets an opening to a street imagined collectively to be in Venice. In other words, for Venice to become on stage it must begin from a street. What *The Merchant of Venice* gives on stage are many streets, then houses, then the courtrooms to conjure a mental picture of the city.

The street in Act 1 Scene 1 emerges as a space of friendship that shares and understands concerns about business and love. The text indicates that Scene 3 is in a "public place" where Bassanio meets Shylock to decide on the terms of loan upon which the plot develops. How is this place different from the street? The place is apparently very near the bourse for just before Antonio enters Shylock winds up his comment on eating with Christians asking for news on the Rialto. Rightly then, Shylock and Antonio talk to each other in the language of the marketplace on their practice as businessmen. It is in this space that Antonio says that "This Hebrew will turn Christian: he grows kind" (1. 3. 179). A business deal that starts in a public place prophetically ends in another public space, the court, where Shylock's forced conversion to Christianity ends Act 4.

There are many scenes strung together between the bourse and the courtroom that are located either in streets, garden, or in the avenue to Portia's house. A survey of these scenes will enlighten us on the way the play is located on stage. Act 2 has nine scenes of which scenes 2, 4, 5, 6 and 8 are all in the streets. Act 3 has five scenes with 1, and 3 in streets and 4 in a garden. Act 4 Scene 1 is in the courtroom and scene 2 is again in a street. The only scene in Act 5 is in the avenue to Portia's house.

The events that unfold in the play are by no means public. They have to do with the execution of a will, a marriage that is in accordance to the will, a loan agreement, apparent loss of property due to shipwreck, elopement, personal loss, default of payment, and animosity between two men, which comes out in the open in the court scene. But then, all the while the dislike that Shylock has for Antonio and what this merchant and his friends think of Shylock is played out in the public space they form. It will not be possible to discount the fact that all the personal events listed come out in the open space of the street. And that is perhaps how the play generates dramatic interest. The city of Venice thus emerges in London suburbs to play out the dramatic mixing of romance with the crucial cultural question of religious tolerance and the nature of justice.

But how does the street emerge in a much later play known for its violent passion? *Othello* took the Elizabethan audience to the streets of Venice in 1602-03 almost seven years after Shylock's appearance on stage. Unlike the space of friendship and love that the earlier play generated in the beginning, this play proclaims slander and treachery in the streets of Venice and later in Cyprus. Here also the creation of the streets that make up the city opens the play on stage. The street continuously plays the drama of concealment and revelation in different ways. For instance, Roderigo evokes a very secretive street in the first word uttered, that opens the play. Roderigo's "Tush!" spoken in the street sets up not just the nature of the action in the play; it creates a space of scheming, darkness, and slander that spirals up to reach the private space of the bedroom of the senator Brabantio.

When Brabantio opens the window and asks the reason for the "terrible summons," a dramatic link is established between the public and the private space. Quite obviously, Roderigo and Iago shout from across the street so that not just Brabantio hears that his daughter has run away, but the whole neighbourhood is woken up to Iago's words, "I am one sir, that comes to tell you, your daughter and the Moor are now making the beast with two backs." The overwhelming of the private space in the public here is what the play continuously effects right through to the moment of the death of Othello. The opening street-scene is structurally the master-scene that provides the cue revealing Iago's slander and mischief which itself is apparently based on his not being made Othello's lieutenant. At this point, it is useful to remember that the whole neighbourhood, given the theatricality of willing suspension of disbelief, is the spectators who would be jostling each other to catch every word that the two rogues utter.

Othello is then a play that is entirely in the public sphere. This is one play where the street with all its sewers and waste and dissipation takes on certain anthropomorphic qualities precisely in the person who would gladly "change [his] humanity with a baboon" (1.3.319). Wherever Iago goes, he takes the street with him. He is the sewer and nuisance ground where Othello walks with his bride. The entire action of the play is, metaphorically speaking, located in the slimy and contagious space known in the play not as Venice, but Iago. Unlike city streets, this space has specific intentions that play with the leisure and privacy of individuals who are exposed to it. In this space, Othello accuses Desdemona of being a strumpet, the Moor puts out the light of his life; the contagion spreads to the extent of destroying the private space of marital bliss.

That is to say, the overwhelming of the private space in the public with which the play opens reaches a stage where there is no private space left. In metaphorical terms, this is yet another expression of the street in the play. This is also a comment on the absence of private space rendered in dramatic terms. For, Iago is the only character who is present in all the scenes in the play excepting only Act 2 Scene 2 where there is Othello's proclamation read by the Herald. No other character appears in this scene. The titular hero is absent, for instance, in Act 3 Scene 1. In such an overwhelming presence of the street, Othello meets Desdemona, but never his wife. The only occasion when he meets his wife after his trance and rage in a state of emotional fit is in Act 5 Scene 2 in the Bedchamber Scene where he smothers her. The drama in this spatial elaboration of character, action and emotions that culminate in the enclosed space of the bedchamber is the moment of recognition for the spectators of the opening of the play. The play, in a sense, addresses then the unique way in which the stage embodies human and other spaces.

How does a play embody the dead body of a public figure in a public space? Shakespeare does not address this "body" in a public space in his major tragedies or the histories. Caesar is perhaps the only hero in Shakespeare who dies in public space and continues to shape the public space and imagine a nation. And so, I propose to address this question with the Roman tragedy *Julius Caesar*. Julius Caesar is assassinated halfway into the play in Act 3 Scene 1. Here again, the play opens in a street in Rome where Flavius scolds the commoners for assembling there. This is preparatory for the entry of Julius Caesar in Scene 2 in a public place. Scene 3 opens in a street with thunder and lightning as the conspirators meet. In Act 2, Scenes 3 and 4 are in the street. The presence of Artemidorous in Scene 3 is to warn Caesar of Brutus; in the next scene, Portia is much concerned about Brutus and Caesar and is eager to know what would happen in the senate. Caesar passes the crowd in front of the Capitol, does not listen to Artemidorous and enters the senate.

A fair surmise is that the play weaves in the fatal connection between the street and Caesar. It is important to remember that Caesar refuses the coronet thrice in the marketplace. That is clearly an instance of Caesar making the street his political space linking his destiny with the citizens. The public esteem of Caesar that grew with the refusal of the coronet in the marketplace haunt the conspirators and makes the senate a bloody space. It is useful to note that though unlike the street, the senate house is an interesting public space because that is where the representatives of the people meet. It is a meeting place for people to exchange ideas, take decisions, and most importantly, one hears the voice of the people. In the play, the senate becomes a space of crime. Clearly, with the assassination, the marketplace does not refuse Caesar. The relationship that the play builds up between the public figure and the public space, especially the street and marketplace, speaks unwittingly as Caesar falls. It is the dramatic realization of this space that Shakespeare elaborates in the funeral oration scene. Cinna is the first to speak in jubilation. He says, "Liberty! Freedom! Tyranny is dead!/Run hence, proclaim, cry it about the streets" (3. 1. 78-79).

But the one who proclaims the story of the assassination in public is Mark Antony. That is how after the assassination, the milling crowd recognizes Caesar as a public figure who was always in their presence as Antony makes his rhetorical extermination of the conspirators, singling out Brutus. Obviously, Caesar is always in the public space. The play makes him the public figure that makes other public figures and their history. His body lies in state in the market place and decides the nature of the emotional configuration of that space.

Mark Antony's funeral oration is the birth of another public figure who knew, like Caesar, the dynamics of the marketplace. Antony reminds the audience on stage and off stage that he had presented a kingly crown to Caesar thrice on the Lupercal that he refused. He is the dramatic space for the bloodied garment that covered Caesar remembering the scene and sequence of offering the crown. In drama couched in rhetoric that builds up an agitated public space, he offers the body of Caesar to the citizens in the form of his will. The presentation of the will and the oration is Antony's creation of a political space in the marketplace that makes him the only friend of Caesar who could inherit his mantle. The play then is making a radical political statement about the body politic of public spaces and the different modulations with which it generates spatial experiences at the level of spectator and stage.

It might then be possible to argue that Shakespeare's theatre was radical, not just for the characterization, or the very many themes that critics seem to identify. His scripts repeatedly examine the material presence of the human body in the spatial experience of emotional moments lived in the daily commerce of telling stories. The space that the script creates in the course of the performance is always of that moment and nothing more. They are performances that approximate the commerce that brought his audience to the dramatization of the history of the human body.

Works Cited

Beckerman, Bernard. *Shakespeare at the Globe 1599-1609*. New York: Collier Books, 1966.

Best, Michael. *Shakespeare's Life and Times*. Internet Shakespeare Editions, University of Victoria: Victoria, BC, 2001-2005. 19 Feb. 2009 <http://ise.uvic.ca/Library/SLT>

Fong Cheang, Wai "Comic Spaces in Shakespeare's History Plays." *NTU Studies in Language and Literature* 18 (2007): 145-166.

Greenblatt, Stephen. *Will in the World: How Shakespeare became Shakespeare*. New York: Norton, 2004.

Johnson, Samuel. "Preface to Shakespeare." <http://shakespeare.palomar.edu/Editors/johnsonpreface.htm>

McManaway, James G. "Introduction." *Shakespeare's Globe Playhouse*. London: Peter Owen, 1963: i-xiii.

Shakespeare, William. *The Merchant of Venice. The Complete Works of William Shakespeare*. London, New York, Toronto: Oxford UP, 1955: 192-216.

______________ . *The Tragedy of King Richard II. The Complete Works of William Shakespeare*: 381-408.

______________ . *The First Part of King Henry IV. The Complete Works of William Shakespeare*: 409-437.

______________ . *The Life of King Henry V. The Complete Works of William Shakespeare*: 470-501.

______________ . *Julius Caesar. The Complete Works of William Shakespeare*: 820-845.

______________ . *Othello: The Moor of Venice. The Complete Works of William Shakespeare*: 943-974.

3

Power of Magic and Magic of Power: Re-reading Shakespeare's *The Tempest* through Strategies of Colonialism and Imperialism

— Baniprata Goswami

Interpretations of *The Tempest* in the last fifty years or so have cast serious concentration on one major issue, that is, Caliban, or more specifically, Prospero's treatment of Caliban. Anyone familiar with the text, knows it very well that Prospero's story is not the only story of the play. Prospero considers Caliban "a thing of darkness," "a dull thing" (1.2.285), "a freckled whelp hag born/ not honour'd with a human shape" (1.2.283-4). Initially Prospero treated Caliban with "human care." He accommodated him in his own cell, and his daughter Miranda "took pains to make him speak," taught him her words and her language. But the profit Caliban reaped out of this was that he learnt how to curse, and he attempted "to violate the honour" of Prospero's child, with a plan to "people" the isle with more Calibans.

The "white man's burden" thus growing too heavy to bear any more, Prospero changes his strategy of treatment and says in Act 1 Scene 2:

> Hagseed, hence!
> Fetch us in fuel; and be quick, thou'rt best
> To answer other business. Shrug'st thou, malice?
> If thou neglect'st, or does unwillingly
> What I command, I'll rack thee with old cramps
> Fill all thy bones with aches, make thee roar
> That beasts shall tremble at thy din. (367-73)

This is Shakespeare's magic "construction" of Prospero, which simultaneously responds to the underlying colonial and cultural anxiety and deconstructs the "benevolent Whiteman." Caliban has been maltreated by the "superior" culture from the beginning of the play. In lieu of his "boundless hospitality to the exiles on their arrival," he was given language. But the gift of language, as Brown shows,

> also inscribes a power relation as he is hailed and recognizes himself as a linguistic subject of the master language. Caliban's refusal marks him as obdurate yet he must voice this in a curse in the language of civility, representing himself as a subject of what he so accurately describes as "Your language." Whatever Caliban does with this gift announces his capture by it. (Brown 144)

Then Prospero appears in the role of a teacher in the uninhabited island, a *tabula rasa*. Ironically his mission is to erase all past from Caliban's mind, to make it another perfect *tabula rasa,* where the white man will cultivate and reap profit. Two children grow side by side, Miranda and Caliban, under the same authority. But Prospero's narrative operates to produce them in "binary division" (Brown 144), one malleable, the other

incorrigible. Miranda is miraculously modest and pure. Caliban is cannibalistic, rough, arrogant, the savage incarnate. Prospero's function thus turns out to be "divide and rule." He arrogates to Miranda all that is cultured and needs protection, and to Caliban all that is debased and rapacious.

Caliban is ugly. He does not have a human shape and is indeed half fish, half ape. He is presented in Prospero's narrative, virtually as the mythical "other," a subject of inferior culture, who should not only subjugate but resign his legitimate claim upon the island and confer it to the higher authority of Prospero. But Caliban is unwilling to commit to this. Within his limitations, he challenges Prospero: "This island's mine, by Sycorax my mother/Which thou tak'st from me" (1. 2. 331-2). And Prospero, unable to answer back, brings from his memory, the charge of rape:

Thou most lying slave
Whom stripes may move, not kindness! I have us'd thee,
Filth as thou art, with human care, and lodg'd thee
In mine own cell, till thou didst seek to violate
The honour of my child. (1. 2. 346-50)

Caliban, "terribly alone" in the island has the legitimate urge to "people the island with more Calibans." But it is an abhorred sin, though when Prospero, the father, himself makes the design and accordingly, sets Miranda free as a trap to catch Ferdinand, the worthy, would be son-in law, definitely not discarding the possibility of having in time "more Ferdinands" that is to be seen only as the civilized "mission." The colonial discourse of "legitimacy" is well exposed in this, that, anyhow, Caliban is to be marked as a "black rapist," for, as Brown shows, it yields a number of advantages:

> The first effect is to circumvent Caliban's version of events by re-encoding his boundlessness as rapacity: his inability to discern a concept of private, bounded property concerning his own dominions is reinterpreted as a desire to violate the chaste virgin, who epitomizes courtly property. Second the capacity to divide and order is shown to be the prerogative of the courtly ruler alone. Third, the memory legitimizes Prospero's takeover of power. (Brown 145)

It is interesting to note that Prospero is not shown to punish Caliban for this offence on the spot, when he is caught red-handed. Everything is reported to the audience when he orders the "poisonous slave" (1. 2. 321) to fetch things for daily work. A man of Prospero's temper might well have killed Caliban for this offence and could have successfully proven that action lawful too, simply in the name of his "superior power" and "fair justice" of his culture. But Prospero does not do this. Prospero's purpose is not only to snatch the sceptre from Caliban, nor is he anxious to justify this by bringing the charge of rape, but his real interest is to build up a scheme that can render strength and duration to his regime. He is not satisfied in exploiting the colony and the colonized as a simple coloniser. He is more intent to ensure permanent domination and control there like an imperialist. That is why Caliban is to be endured and not killed or eliminated. The dominant White culture can hate him, can torment him, but can never miss him. For, Caliban does the work. Caliban is labour. Prospero enlightens Miranda:

> But as 'tis
> We cannot miss him; he does make our fire
> Fetch in our wood, and serves in offices
> That profit us. (1.2.312-5)

Profit, the single word then, exposes the true purpose of Prospero and undercuts the simple colonial reading of the play for matters more serious. As long as Prospero restrains his activities only in the takeover of territory, appropriation of material resources, exploitation of labour and interference with political and cultural structure of another territory or nation, he plays the role of a colonist or colonial master. Colonial operation has its own methodology and is never philanthropic, as Jorge Klor de Alva's analysis shows in the following lines:

> In most places, the original inhabitants, who logically grouped themselves into separate cultural units [ethnicities], all but disappeared after contact, wiped out physically by disease and abuse, and later, genetically and socially by miscegenation, and lastly, culturally, by the religious and political practices of the Europeans and their mixed progeny. Even in the regions where native peoples survived as corporate groups in their own greatly transformed communities, especially in the core areas of Mesoamerica and the Andes, within two or three generations they were greatly reduced in number and politically and socially marginalized from the new centers of power. (243)

The political and cultural transformation of Caliban, which is attempted by Prospero and his civilizing mission, is no doubt a threat. But the moment "profit" comes into the issue, Prospero grows into a capitalist and his colonialism makes way for imperialism.

It is true that imperialism, in its most popular sense, is seen as a "global system" that grew up to capture and monopolize market for European industry and finance capital, a project which, however, was achieved through colonial domination. Thus, imperialism, in one sense, becomes the highest stage of capitalism, as Lenin sees it, and on the other, it becomes the highest stage of colonialism too. It is thus both, an economic as well as political system of penetration, control, exploitation and rule, ensuring profit in every possible way.

Another useful way of distinguishing between imperialism and colonialism, however, is to separate them in spatial terms, and to consider imperialism, as Loomba suggests, to be a phenomenon originating in the Metropolis, the process which opens new vistas of domination and control in the colony. "What happens in the colonies as a consequence of imperial domination is colonialism or neo-colonialism" (Loomba 12).

Factory, industry and finance capital do not transpire in *The Tempest* actively. But that cannot prevent the entry of imperialism in the play at large. For, Prospero's colonial operation in the island, after all, has a prehistory, and itself is not the cause, but the effect of a larger motive. For twelve years he cannot forget his revenge and waits patiently for the final hour. As the Metropolis, Milan is the starting point of the play and the re-capture of that usurped dukedom of Milan is the chief endeavour of Prospero's project. Caliban, or colonialism, so to say, is his mere pastime.

Barker and Hulme in their analysis of the play, have referred to the boatswain's angry dismissal of the nobles to their cabins in the first scene of the play, and commented that, though itself not a rebellious act according to the then custom of the sea, the incident "offers a shadow of considerable disturbance in the normal hierarchy of power relation" (198). Accordingly, Antonio usurps Prospero's dukedom of Milan, Prospero usurps Caliban's legitimate claim over the island, Caliban attempts to rape Prospero's daughter and revolt against Prospero. To Barker and Hulme, this series of action "is the play" (198).

But this "power thirst" interestingly grows into a "power threat" in no other character but Prospero, and in his merciless exercise of power in order to achieve control and authority and self justification, he becomes an imperialist. Prospero, the colonialist, exploits and tortures; Prospero, the imperialist, legitimizes this torture and connects it to the larger purpose of monopolizing profit and political domination, a means to accomplish the even larger goal of reaching the centre of undisputed power, where no humane consideration can ever disturb him. The colonizer is an ugly torturer, but still a man, aware and careful of the counter struggle, the resistance, and its related "anxiety." But the imperialist is simply a demon, despotic in his monopoly of power and determined for his total domination and control.

Prospero shows this in his treatment of Miranda, whom he suspects to doubt his story and finally revolt, when he roars back at appealing Miranda, "what! I say,/My foot my tutor?" (1.2.469-70). It is not the father but that ugly, self loving demon, which comes out. And his treatment of Ariel particularly crosses all limits. Ariel's only guilt was to seek liberty. But imperialism can never dispense with a skilled labour. It is through him that it exploits. It is he whom it exploits. Prospero does not know magic, he has not learnt any thing, seize of his books can kill his art; even Caliban knows this. He tells Stephano, "Remember/First to possess his books; for without them/He's but a sot" (3.2.99-101). Prospero's capital is his unchallenged power, with which he threatens Ariel at every opportunity, so that Ariel does the entire work and Prospero gets the credit of the magician:

Prospero:	Dost thou forget From what a torment I did free thee?
Ariel:	No.
Prospero:	Thou dost, and think'st much to tred the ooze. . .
Ariel:	I do not, sir.
Prospero:	Thou liest, malignant thing! Hast thou forgot The foul witch Sycorax. . .
Ariel:	No, sir.
Prospero:	Thou hast. . . .
Ariel:	I thank thee, master.
Prospero:	If thou more murmur'st, I will rend an oak And peg thee in his knotty entrails, till Thou hast howl'd away twelve winters.
Ariel:	Pardon, master. (1.2.250-96)

Prospero ruthlessly reminds Ariel of his indebtedness to the master, an act of memory which it is necessary to repeat periodically (1.2.261-2). "This constant reminding," as Brown affirms, "operates as a mode of symbolic violence: what is really at issue is the underlining of a power relation. Ariel is, paradoxically, bound in service by this constant reminder of Prospero's gift of freedom to him" (143). Prospero makes use of the memory of the previous regime of Sycorax as an evil other, in contrast to which his own regime appears to be only ostensibly better. For, though Ariel had been confined by Sycorax "Into a cloven pine: within which rift/Imprison'd thou didst painfully remain/A dozen years" (1.2.277-9), he had not been subject to hard toil, as he had been under Prospero. Even Prospero's promise of release seems to be nothing more than a lie. "Thou did promise/ To bate me a full year" (1.2.249-50), he says to Ariel, but in fact has been taking his service for longer period. Obviously he freed Ariel twelve years ago, when he had arrived in the island but is now unwilling to release him before his purpose is fulfilled.

Above all, it is this merciless and shameless usurpation of Ariel's skill and labour, extracted through threat and fury that makes Prospero appear an imperialist. Magic is airy nothing, a sugar coated disguise for power and exploitation. This is as true in Prospero as in the contemporary feel good air of globalization. Prospero wins, globalization also wins, at least, so it seems. But the question remains as to how long Prospero will continue to win.

At the end of *The Tempest*, Prospero leaves his art for greater power and Ariel, still harassed, is commanded to ensure the wind for the safe and easy journey back to Milan. But if Ariel wakes up, if multitudes of Ariels and Calibans and their millions of spelled friends in the world wake up, there is every possibility that another tempest will appear, more fierce and beyond all control. Do we hear its upcoming roar?

Works Cited

Barker and Hulme. '"Nymphs and Reapers heavily vanish': The Discursive Con-texts of *The Tempest."Alternative Shakespeares.* Vol. I. Ed. John Drakakis. London: Routledge, 1985: 192-99.

Brown, Paul. "'This thing of darkness I acknowledge mine': *The Tempest* and the Discourse of Colonialism." *Political Shakespeare: New Essays in Cultural Materialism.* Ed. Jonathan Dollimore and Alan Sinfield. London: Manchester University Press, 1985: 141-47.

Griffiths, Trevor R. "'This island mine': Caliban and Colonialism." *YES* 13(1983): 163-9.

Jorge Klor de Alva. "'The Postcolonization of the (Latin) American Experience: A Reconsideration of "Colonialism," "Postcolonialism" and "Mestizaje."' *After Colonialism, Imperial Histories and Postcolonial Displacement*. Ed. G. Prakash. Princeton, NJ: Princeton University Press: 238-249.

Loomba, Ania. "Seizing the Book." In *The Tempest,* New Casebook Edition. Ed. R. S. White. London, 1999: 138-157.

Shakespeare, William. *The Tempest*. Ed. Frank Kermode. London: Methuen, 1954.

4

Power, Dominance and Survival in Shakespeare's Last Plays

— Raju Parghi

Shakespeare's philosophy of life, portrayed in his plays, is universal. His plays continue to offer various horizons of interpretations, diverse ways of understanding and a range of significances in the twenty-first century. The last plays include *Pericles, Cymbeline, The Winter's Tale* and *The Tempest*. Some critics have termed them as romances and some others have labelled them as tragicomedies. Apart from *The Tempest,* the other three plays have received less attention from the critics, intellectuals and scholars across the globe. Nevertheless, they are excellent pieces knitting together history, romance, tragic events and happy endings.

The primary focus of this paper is to highlight our instinct for domination and drive for survival. *The Tempest* has been interpreted from postcolonial perspectives by many critics focusing on the struggle and sustaining of power; this is true of the other three plays. Pericles's struggles to reunite with his daughter in *Pericles,* Cymbeline's reluctance to marry his daughter to Posthumus in *Cymbeline* and Leontes' suspicion of his wife Hermione in *The Winter's Tale*—all the actions create uneasiness and fear only to settle down happily at the end.

The paper aims to interpret these plays in terms of politics of power, dominance and survival placing *The Tempest* at the centre. Mention is also made on the artistic superiority of *The Tempest* over the other three plays. The chronological order of the Last Plays is as follows: *Pericles* (1607-08), *Cymbeline* (1609-10), *The* to seize power with their malice and false ambition but remain unfulfilled. They lack the required potentials to be leaders. But Shakespeare's creation of Prospero is something unique as "he knew that every energetic dealer with the world must seek a sincere and liberal pardon for many things" (Palmer 66). He forgives and perhaps is at best in his new political beginning.

In *The Winter's Tale* and *Pericles* the driving force for power is not from "outside" but from "within." There is no threat to anyone as ruler but the struggle arises from within the individual. In *Pericles,* authority is used to hide hypocrisy, to bury the truth under the carpet and to punish the innocent; while in *The Winter's Tale* Leontes misuses his power only to shame his wife Hermione publicly having accused her of infidelity. His position as king with monopolized power makes him blind to truth while he suffers from his own suspicion and sexual jealousy. In *Pericles,* the entire action of the play revolves around the riddle that Antiochus, King of Antioch, puts before the princes, if answered would be suitor to his daughter, only to forbid his daughter to get married. This is the riddle:

> I am no viper, yet I feed
> On mother's flesh which did me breed.
> I sought a husband, in which labour
> I found that kindness in a father:
> He's father, son, and husband mild,
> I mother, wife, and yet his child.
> How they may be, and yet in two,
> As you will live, resolve it you. (1. 1. 64-70)

Identifying in its meaning an incestuous relationship between daughter and the father, Pericles remains silent as he discerns the mind of the king: he would be killed in either way. Pericles's decision to quit Tyre befriends him with Cleon, the Governor of Tharsus providing him with grains to stop the starvation and famine in the kingdom. Overcoming the storm in the sea and rescued by fate and time, Pericles with the support of the fishermen, wins the heart of Thiasa, the daughter of Simionides, king of Pentapolis at the bride's tournament. A worthy leader and chivalrous man, Pericles's thirst for power to become the King of

Both Antonio and Sebastian rely on "chance" and try to seize the kingdom; the former succeeds in doing so before the play opens. Sebastian follows Antonio's advice and prepares himself to kill his ailing, tired and pain struck brother, Alonso. Sebastian tells Antonio:

> Thy case, dear friend,
> Shall be my precedent; as thou got'st Milan
> I'll come by Naples. Draw thy sword: one stroke
> Shall free thee the tribute which thou pay'st.
> And I the king shall love thee. (2.1. 290-294)

Sebastian does not succeed to fulfil his evil intention as Ariel, Prospero's spirit, wakes Gonzalo up in order to stop them. Even Gonzalo at a time dreams of a utopian kingdom if he gets to rule the island, though his intention is not wickedness. His philosophy of power and rule is "all things to all people." He says to Antonio, "I would with such perfection govern sir, to excel the golden age" (2.1.174). The utopian dream remains a dream for Gonzalo, but the greedy, ambitious and villainous nature of Antonio and Sebastian leads to conflict. Prospero's practice of black magic has dual purpose: one to teach a lesson to his brother Antonio and the other is to get Miranda married to Ferdinand. He casts a spell on the ship in which Alonso, Sebastian, Antonio, Gonzalo, Ferdinand and others travel back to Naples after having attended Alonso's daughter's marriage.

In *Cymbeline,* the desire for power works in the mind of the queen who wants Cloten marry Imogen (step-daughter) in order to rule after Cymbeline's death or to kill Imogen so that Cloten and herself can be the heir of the kingdom as she despises the king and plots against Imogen. The queen tells Cloten:

> . . . gone she is
> To death or to dishonour, and my end
> Can make good use of either: she being down,
> I have the placing of the British crown. (3. 5. 62-65)

The Tempest and *Cymbeline* share a common motive on politics as weaklings like Antonio, Sebastian, the Queen and Cloten attempt

Winter's Tale (1610-11) and *The Tempest* (1611). These plays are "accretion of unforeseen new possibilities" (Clemen 218). They portray a constant struggle between good and evil, kindness and selfishness, innocence and guilt, faith (loyalty) and suspicion, life and death—the known fears and the unknown.

It is universally known that man is a political and social animal. From birth to death, in one or the other form, human innate nature is of domination, be it king or servant, rich or poor. The Last Plays of Shakespeare, though are considered as romances dealing with love, marriage, peace and forgiveness, yet they can be looked at as instances of constant struggle for power, impulse for dominance, and longing for survival. The struggle for power is either hereditary or sudden, but always vaulting and ruthless. A strong desire to rule at any cost not only corrupts personality but leads to dangerous consequences and conflict. "They transform patriarchal hierarchies into a state of disorder" (Dollimore 111).

Prospero in *The Tempest,* as the name suggests, only prospers wherever he is. Though dethroned and cheated by his brother Antonio, Prospero still remains a ruler, albeit of the scarcely inhabited island where destiny leads him. He tells Miranda, "Twelve years since, Miranda twelve years,/Thy father was the Duke of Milan and/Prince of power" (1. 2. 52-54).

Prospero's negligence of his kingdom and his growing interest, like Faustus, in the books and black magic which he prizes above the dukedom, create an opportunity for his ambitious and villainous brother Antonio to dethrone him and take control over the kingdom as the new Duke of Milan. The villainy grows higher as he suggests and tempts Sebastian, the brother of Alonso, king of Naples, to smother him in his sleep and crown himself as the king. He insinuates Sebastian saying:

O! What might?—No More:—
And yet methinks I see it in thy face,
What thou shouldst be: the occasion speaks thee; and
My strong imagination sees a crown
Dropping upon thy head. (2. 1. 204-208)

Tyre and his decision to return to Tyre costs him dearly as he loses (gets separated) from both his wife and new born daughter in the storm at sea. For him political accountability is much more important than family responsibility. But then, the reunion with his daughter and wife after fourteen years, "the political world at last will be ordered as two kingdoms are united: Perilces and Thaisa rule in one and Marina and Lysimachus in the other" (Moore 42).

The Winter's Tale has sharp resemblance to *Othello* as the action of the play expands over the self-ignited suspicion and sexual jealousy of Leontes over his wife Hermione. In the words of E. Dowden, in this play "thought is more rapid than the language." Leontes is not convinced with the unfolding of the innocence of his wife. He is responsible for the sorrowful events that befall him. Ellen Terry calls him a convincing portrait of a jealous man than Othello. His political power and authority bring him to test as he, like a misogynist, first accuses Hermione of infidelity and later even discards his new born daughter. The threat to his kingdom arises when he learns from the oracle that he himself is guilty:

> Hermione is chaste; Polixenes blameless; Camillo a true subject; Leontes a jealous Tyrant; his innocent babe truly begotten; and the king shall live without an heir, if that which is lost be not found. (3. 2. 132-137)

This oracular revelation becomes true as his son Mamillius pines for the queen and eventually dies. As Leontes orders the new babe to be thrown into the wilderness he is left without heir. His political life appears dim; and encounters danger as he learns from Paulina that Hermione too could not survive the shock of her son's death. Leontes's political power and dominance appear bleak as he loses interest and burns in purgatory of guilt. The transition of uncertainty and wonder takes place as Leontes finds his lost heir and his wife Hermione only revealing that his political life would continue along with the reunion of the family. Bristol remarks:

> *The Winter's Tale* may speak to a social desire for healing and redress of grievance. But Leontes' murderous folly has had

> irrevocable consequences not only for himself but for others. It is not altogether clear that the embrace of husband and wife in the final scene can be adequate compensation to Hermione for the loss of her son or for the time that she has spent waiting for the return of Perdita. (172)

In *The Winter's Tale* and *Pericles* the power and dominance of an individual over the kingdom is sustained only when there is reunion of the respective individual's family. The loss of heir leads towards the elimination of political authority. *The Tempest* and *Cymbeline* too share some unexpected endings as Cymbeline gets back his lost sons and accepts his daughter's marriage with Posthumus, while *The Tempest* rides on Prospero's forgiveness of Antonio, the domination and power of individual continues behind some unexpected and miraculous happenings. John Keats rightly remarks, ". . . it struck me, what quality went to form a Mass of Achievement, especially in literature, and Shakespeare possessed so enormously— I mean 'Negative Capability' that is when a man capable of being in uncertainties, mysteries, doubts, without any irritable reaching after fact and reason" (quoted in Andrews 46).

The Last Plays can also be analyzed as plays with strong spirit of survival. In the romances, "the protagonist must travel, be shipwrecked or be lost. The movement of the plot is from sorrow to joy, from division to unity" (McEvoy 242). Unlike tragedies these romances focus on to live life in peace and harmony, truth and brotherhood. They highlight a simple logic of life: live and let others live. This spirit of survival can be elaborated further as spirit of reconciliation, forgiveness, reunion and compromise.

In the spiritual sense of survival these plays grow from sin to suffering to salvation, a kind of spiritual journey like Dante's Inferno, Purgatorio and Paradiso in *The Divine Comedy*. The action of the Last Plays also revolves around tension/conflict/sin. The self-invited suspicion and sexual jealousy of Leontes; incest committed by Antiochus and his daughter; Pericles's abandoning his daughter and wife (thought dead); Antonio's action to dethrone his brother Prospero; Prospero's illegal domination over Caliban and his island are the individual deeds considered to be sinful, a kind of Inferno. The lengthy period of suffering of sixteen years in *The Winter's Tale*, fourteen years in *Pericles* and twelve years in *The Tempest;* Cymbeline's realization of truth, the misdeed done by the Queen could be considered as suffering of the individual—a kind of journey through Purgatory. The journey of uncertainty and suffering finally leads to new life towards reconciliation and forgiveness, their reunion with the beloved/friend/family at the end of the plays resemble a journey to Paradise.

The cycle of sin, suffering and salvation gets completed bringing a change and hope for better living. Many critics have recorded *Pericles, Cymbeline* and *The Winter's Tale* as grounding for *The Tempest.* This is quite mysterious as *The Tempest* does not resemble any other plays of Shakespeare while the former three plays do have resemblances with *King Lear* and *Othello.*

The Tempest is artistically superior as it does not divert from the plot. The play is filled to overflowing with happiness as no one is killed; everyone survives the calamities and experiences forgiveness. It celebrates life, while *The Winter's Tale, Cymbeline,* and *Pericles* portray the loss of life. Amidst power struggle and survival the hierarchy of power politics continues, the families split and reunite, only to reveal that love of power/leadership/politics is more important than family.

Works Cited

Andrews W.T. Ed. *Readings in Literary Criticism: Critics on Shakespeare.* New Delhi: Universal Book Stall, 1991.

Bristol, Michael. *Big Time Shakespeare.* London and New York: Routledge, 1996.

Cleon, Wolfgang. *The Development of Shakespeare's Imagery.* Second edition. London and New York: Methuen, 1972.

Dollimore, Jonathan and Alan Sinfield. *Political Shakespeare: Essays in Cultural Materialism.* Second edition. Madras: T.R. Publications, 1995.

McEvoy, Sean. *Shakespeare: The Basics.* London and New York: Routledge, 2002.

Palmer, D.J. Ed. *Shakespeare: The Tempest.* London: Macmillan, 1991.

Moore, Jeanie Grant. "Kingship and Kinship in *Pericles.*" *Rocky Mountain Modern Language Association* 57.1(2003): 33-48.

Shakespeare, William. "Cymbeline." *Illustrated Stratford Shakespeare.* Hungary: Chancellor Press, 1982: 924-953.

______________ . "Pericles, The Prince of Tyre." *Illustrated Stratford Shakespeare*. Hungary: Chancellor Press, 1982. 954-972.

______________ . "The Tempest." *Illustrated Stratford Shakespeare.* Hungary: Chancellor Press, 1982. 9-29.

______________ . "The Winter's Tale." *Illustrated Stratford Shakespeare.* Hungary: Chancellor Press, 1982. 329-349.

5

Shakespeare: A Capitalist?

— Harini Jeyaraman and K.Sreena

The rise of Marxist criticism during the nineteenth century led to new interpretations of art and literature. The writings that were hitherto considered to be great pieces of literature were subjected to revaluation and found to be either extremely worthy or entirely worthless. The influence of Marxist literary criticism on Shakespeare's works can be traced back to the Victorian age. When Shakespeare is studied in the light of this criticism, the reader is confronted with the question of interpreting his texts sans his own personality; and perhaps, this dichotomy has led to several studies. One such work is Edward Bond's *Bingo,* which is a revisionist reading of Shakespeare's world and works. The main thrust of Bond's criticism on Shakespeare is that Shakespeare never tried to explore the realities of his time, but solely depended on the historical facts. Bond has a deep admiration for Shakespeare's intellectual strength and passionate beauty, but rejects him for the compromise that he made on the stage.

However, there are a few critics belonging to the same school of thought expressing a different view which interprets Shakespeare as a dramatist who depicted the realities of the society of his time. He would not have tried his hand in bringing about a social change but he certainly holds a mirror up to life through his characters.

This paper attempts to read Shakespeare in two different perspectives of Marxist School of criticism; first, Shakespeare as a man of his time, and the other, Shakespeare as the dramatist of all times. First part of the paper discusses Shakespeare's life solely based on Edward Bond's play, *Bingo.* It will be injustice to approach a great dramatist of all time without looking into his contributions to the world of literature. Suitably, the second part of the paper is close reading of Shakespeare's plays as a product of the Renaissance humanism.

Shakespeare: The Man of His Time

"A poet is man speaking to men." —*Wordsworth*

What makes an art form effective? This question has been discussed by many thinkers from the very beginning of the history of art. Spanning from the Aristotelian era to the postmodern or post-theoretical era, thinkers have viewed art differently. In the nineteenth century, Oscar Wilde and other English aesthetic thinkers upheld the concept of "art for art's sake." It goes with the traditional notion of art that is propounded in the works of Shakespeare and other Elizabethan and classical writers. There was another school of criticism during the Victorian period, a school led by John Ruskin. This school of critics considered art, literature and criticism as an expression of those ideas and ideals which ennobled, and enlightened life and society. For them art stands for life's sake; art is also subservient to morality.

The Marxist school of critics extended this notion to situate literature and art in its ideological, social and cultural environment. All forms of art are either the product or producers of culture and ideology in any society. While the traditional Marxist critics like Lukas and others strictly followed the conventional Marxist notion of art as a social product, the post-Marxist thinkers like Adorno, Brecht extended the forms of art to other disciplines. Raymond Williams, among other critics, moved far away and preferred culture to ideology. He felt that Marxist critics unduly separated the economical aspects from the cultural and overlooked individuals.

Theodor Adorno, the French Marxist critic, in his essay "Commitment", points out the essentiality of social responsibility in a writer. He differentiates the autonomous text from the committed text. The autonomous text is the imaginative creation of a free thinker. A committed work adheres to the realities of its time. History is the material condition in which these texts are produced.

Edward Bond, the Marxist playwright, in his intertextual play on Shakespeare, *Bingo,* questions the social commitment of Shakespeare as a writer. Though he admits Shakespeare's intellectual and passionate beauty, Bond criticizes Shakespeare for his lack of commitment to the social realities of the period. Shakespeare had taken the subject matter for his plays either from history or from familiar characters of his time. Shakespeare's characters and themes are universal archetypes for future authors. The writers of all times either directly or indirectly copy the traits of Shakespearean characters and themes. But he was careless or less concerned about the social, economic and cultural problems of the Renaissance.

Bingo deals with Shakespeare's life after his retirement from the stage. The play centres on a crisis in the town of Stratford, where Shakespeare was born and where he passed his last years. Bond traces the contradictions that Shakespeare had in his life and works: he was a "corrupt seer" and we are a "barbarous civilization." The play dramatizes Shakespeare's response to this challenge in the ordinary life of the town in which he lived. Bond depicts the dramatist who had sympathized with the poor naked wretches in *King Lear* as siding with the ruthless landholders.

For Bond, art is the expression of moral sanity. Shakespeare's plays show this need for sanity and its political expression, justice. But how did he live? His behaviour as a property-owner made him closer to Goneril than Lear. He supported and benefited from the Goneril-society with its prisons, workhouses, whipping, starvation, mutilation, pulpit hysteria and all the rest of it.

An example of this is his role in the Welcombe enclosure. A large part of his income came from rents paid on common fields at Welcombe near Stratford. Some important landowners wanted to enclose these fields—for the reasons given in the play—and there was the risk that the enclosure would affect Shakespeare's rents. He could side either with the landowners or with the poor who would lose their land and livelihood. He sided with landowners. They gave him a guarantee against loss—and this is not a neutral document because it implies that should the people fighting the enclosures come to him for help he would refuse it. The town did write to him for help and he did nothing. The struggle is quite well documented and there is no record of opposition from Shakespeare. He may have doubted that the enclosures would succeed, but at best this means he sat at home with his guarantee while others made the resistance that was the only way to stop them. They were stopped for a time. The fields were not finally enclosed till 1775.

However, in this play about his life, Shakespeare sits in his garden and broods. His wife keeps to her bed and hides from him. The silence of Shakespeare throughout the play reflects his inactivity as a responsible, socially committed artist. He does not react to the happenings around him. The conversation between Combe and Shakespeare explicitly points out this:

> *Combe*: Don't support the town or the tenants. When the council wrote, I ignore them. Be non-committed or say you think nothing will come of it. Stay in your garden. I'll pay for that.
>
> *Shakespeare:* You read too much into it. I'm protecting my own interests. Not supporting you, or fighting the town. (6-7)

In another context Judith, the daughter of Shakespeare says: "He should be happy. No responsibilities. No duties" (11). This attitude is a reminder of the later day Lear. Another characteristic that Bond attributes to Shakespeare is fear. Fear is lack of understanding. Shakespeare's fear is due to his contradiction within himself. He believes in certain values, but society teaches him just the opposite. That is why the world is absurd.

Bond is, however, not a biographer but an artist. In *Bingo*, which Bond subtitles "Scenes of Money and Death," he wants to give expression to some passionately held convictions about the role of the writer in a society. According to Bond, art and life are inseparable. Artist is a person who seeks out morality. But Shakespeare invalidated everything he wrote because he separated art from life.

The question, whether one has to read a writer on the basis of his/her personal life or the historical background in which he or she lived, is left to the judgment of the reader.

Shakespeare: The Dramatist

"Shakespeare was not of an age but of all times."

—*Ben Jonson*

The contention that Shakespeare has not been faithful to the social realities of his time or has not included his society in his works is an accusation that has been existing for quite sometime now, at least since the advent of Marxist criticism during the last century. It is observed that all his plays are either historical or based on the happenings in the distant past and that all his characters generally represent the nobility and the gentry. According to Raymond Williams, "we cannot separate literature and art from other kinds of social practice, in such a way as to make them subject to quite special and distinct laws" (407). Another important critic, Jonathan Dollimore, while discussing the development of cultural materialism mentions the recent development "of a field of work relating literary texts to, for example, the following: enclosures and the oppression of the rural poor; State power and resistance to it; reassessment of what actually were the dominant ideologies of the period . . . " (vii). On the basis of such criticism, there have been strong arguments that in Shakespeare "dominant ideologies" of his period were almost not seen.

Although Shakespeare has been accused of not showing empathy with the common man of his period—as mentioned and portrayed by Edmund Bond in the play *Bingo*—there are other critics like Aleksandr A. Smirnov who have vociferously supported him. In fact, Smirnov has done a systematic study of Shakespeare and his plays, and has brought out a strong counter-argument. He traces the social history of England during the sixteenth and seventeenth centuries and tries to connect it with Shakespeare's plays. In Smirnov's words,

> Shakespeare is the humanist ideologist of the bourgeoisie of the time, for whom the source material of his plays had no importance, and which, as Engels has pointed out, he did not disdain to borrow even from the Middle Ages. He was concerned only with how he could adapt this material. It does not follow that he denied the living present around him, or that he was but another of that group of "closet

> humanists" whom Engels characterized as 'second or third-rate men, or cautious Philistines who are afraid of burning their fingers (like Erasmus).' (16)

The next point of contention is the absence of idealism that was prevalent during his time when the New Age England witnessed renaissance and as a result the fall of feudalism. Smirnov argues every point of criticism thus:

> It would be futile to attempt to find a prescribed morality in Shakespeare. His morality is of a general tenor, not consisting of dogmatic tenets, but of broad rules of conduct. Such is the rule, or principle, of trust in *Hamlet, King Lear,* and, to a lesser extent, in *Coriolanus;* the principle of conscience in *Othello* and *Macbeth;* the principle of mercy in *The Merchant of Venice* and *Measure for Measure,* and so on. Even surpassing these is the principle of the creative love of life, and the heroic struggle for the preservation of its best aspects. (17)

Based on the above observation we may say that Shakespeare drew the material for the concrete expression of these abstract principles from the people of his own generation or had survived in tradition. Smirnov continues:

> Shakespeare does not sermonize; he is never didactic. The moral aspects of each problem and each situation are revealed so forcefully, that the reader is inescapably compelled to draw his own conclusions. In this light, it can be said that Shakespeare's work abounds in moral elements. Accordingly, he elucidates the problems of the individual: his rights, his relations to the family, the state and society, and the race question. He always stresses the social roots of every problem. His conception of society is based on a broad and profound conception of the individual. (25)

The arguments put forth by critics like Smirnov lead us to the question whether art is for art's sake or is it for the society. If an author can live through his works for centuries together, and still enjoy popularity, his/her works should certainly carry the personal conviction and beliefs of the author and they should also hold the mirror up to nature. Considering these facts, we can view

Shakespeare at times as a Capitalist and sometimes not. This is perhaps an inconclusive question and it could be left without an answer for the future generations to read and enjoy an author without probing into his personal leanings.

Works Cited

Bond, Edward. *Bingo*. London: Eyre Methuen, 1974.

Dollimore, Jonathan and Alan Sinfield. *Political Shakespeare*. London: MUP, 1985.

Drakakis, John. "Afterword: the next generation." *Alternative Shakespeare*. Ed. Terence Hawkes. Vol. II. London: Routledge, 1996.

Howard, Jean E. and Marion F. O'Conner, eds. *Shakespeare Reproduced: The Text in History and Ideology*. London: Routledge, 1987.

Smirnov, Aleksandr A. Trans. Sonia Volochova and Kronman Zena Rautbort. *Shakespeare: A Marxist Interpretation*. New York: The Critics Group, 1936.

Williams, Raymond. *Marxism and Literature*. Oxford, UK: OUP, 1977.

6

Living through Future: Shakespeare in the Management Classroom

— Punyashree Panda

With the onset of globalization and free market, literature, especially classical literature, has taken a back seat in the contemporary consciousness. The present day youth would wish to take up a degree in engineering, medicine or management than study the greatness of Shakespeare. If at all they would read a literary text, it would be a Chetan Bhagat or a J.K. Rowling (with no offence meant to either author). Nevertheless, that does not mean Shakespeare is out to lose his relevance in the contemporary scenario or in the future.

However, it has become essential now, more than ever before, that we rediscover Shakespeare and merge him into the present day mould. Teachers of communication who are imaginative and insightful, for example, can shape Shakespeare to fit into the contemporary management classroom. This paper looks into such interesting possibilities and the implications thereof. This paper thus seeks to establish Shakespeare as a modern day communicator in whose writing there are lessons for the future managers of this country and the globe. It also attempts to suggest some stimulating and practicable ideas to enliven the classroom atmosphere with the use of Shakespearean plays.

It is one thing to teach Shakespeare; it is completely another to teach through Shakespeare. For the management classroom, unlike the literature classroom, it becomes important to emphasize the problems and concepts of management that Shakespeare has dealt with in his plays and hence a grouping is required to be achieved between the present-day managerial tasks and the managerial problems and the troubles that Shakespeare's kings and queens faced in his plays.

Before we delve deeper into the teaching of managerial concepts through Shakespeare, it is necessary that we first establish the need of arts as an integral part of management education. Recently, owing to the sub-prime crisis in the United States and the resultant economic meltdown and also owing to corporate scandals as the Satyam fiasco in our country and other corporate scams around the world, a sense of inadequacy has crept into the practices of modern day management education. Ironically, the disgraced chief of Satyam Group was a "product" of Harvard Business School, the Mecca of management education. (I have consciously used the term "product" because that is what the top-notch B-Schools in India as well as the world end up doing to human beings.)

While one needs to keep in mind that all businesses seek profit and profit only, it has now become more necessary than ever that the dignity of human relationships and values are maintained intact when the corporates deal with both their internal as well as external stockholders. Corporate social responsibility has become a buzzword in the business world now thanks to the practices of some companies such as Infosys and Tata, to name a few. Whatever business strategies and policies it may adopt, a company is still run by people and the people, who run it, hence need to be sensitized to the "human condition" as Edward Said would put it. And who better to deal with the human condition than Shakespeare?

Whereas management education follows a highly structured, simulated pattern of teaching and learning, learning management lessons through Shakespeare can increase and broaden the creative boundaries of the future managers. In fact, many reputed B-Schools in the United States and United Kingdom have adopted Shakespeare's plays and students are taught management theories and lessons through the Shakespearean classics. Michael Useem, Professor of Management at the University of Pennsylvania's Wharton School in Philadelphia and the author of a number of books on management including the much acclaimed *The Leadership Moment: Nine True Stories of Triumph and Disaster and Their Lessons for All,* states: "If you wonder why a great literary figure appears front and center in a business school curriculum, it's because our students learn vibrant and indelible lessons from the pen of Sir William Shakespeare" (quoted in Williams: Online)

There are many lessons to be learnt from Shakespeare. Some very specific skills that fit into management education are *stage presence, effective communication,* and *strategic thinking.* Apart from these, *leadership skills, ethics, credibility,* and *integrity* are very vital aspects of modern day business that can be learnt from Shakespeare. Built into the context, Shakespeare's plays can enlighten today's managers on human relation issues as well. It is in fact, the continued relevance of the Shakespearean classics that drives one to apply the lessons from the play for the learning of managerial traits. As Paul Corrigan remarks in the introduction to his very interesting book *Shakespeare on Management: Leadership Lessons for Today's Managers*:

> In Shakespeare's time, the "senior manager" was called a "leader," whose job was to lead a nation, a clan or a country. Leaders were also called kings, queens, dukes or lords. Then, as now, organizations needed leaders; managers either led or failed; and leaders had to worry about managing with limited resources. Good leaders managed their staff well and bad ones badly or not at all. Good managers understood the vital need for information and bad ones ignored it, feeling that communication with subordinates was not necessary. (Corrigan 1)

Let us now dig into some specific plays to find out if these claims are worth the deliberation. Let us take up *Henry V*, where the young prince becomes a king and also an adult rather unexpectedly. As if that is not enough, he also has to lead his forces in a battle. Carol Adelman, an expert on Shakespeare workshops for corporate executives, tells us:

> This scenario illustrates what happens in all organizations, when someone goes from being a colleague to being a boss, from a confined area of responsibility to being responsible for a far wider scope. Both the skill sets and the personal relationships are changed while moving up the organization. (quoted in Williams: Online)

This play also helps the modern day managers understand the very important skills of leadership which can make or mar a modern day business. With the changing magnitude of global business which offers situations of uncertainty and difficulty, a manager needs to act as a leader who can lead and motivate her/his subordinates to excel in business. One of the most important aspects the modern day leader needs to take care of is her/his credibility in the work environment. Kathryn Callahan rightly points out *Henry V* as a play that trains modern day managers on "how to establish credibility as a leader, identify habits that hold you back from achieving your full potential, and unite a disparate group around a common goal" (Callahan: Online).

Another Shakespearean play, *Julius Ceasar,* has lessons to offer on betrayal and power games. A thorough reading of *Julius Caesar* teaches the executive "who's living through a power struggle at the top to recognize the possibilities of the explosiveness of political manoeuvring" (Callahan: Online). The lessons of emotional and political intelligence that *Julius Caesar* can teach management students also include the ability to distinguish and examine people and relationships. It also teaches the manager as to "when openness is appropriate and when it is naive" (Callahan: Online). Managing feelings of betrayal that can arise out of organizational change are difficult to handle and *Julius Caesar* has ample lessons on this managerial aspect as well. Similarly, *Othello* has lessons to offer on the perils of distrust and miscommunication. It teaches the present day manager about the disastrous consequences of misappropriation of facts.

In the context of management education, the case study approach is what really works out well with students. The young manager needs to comprehend aspects of business by analyzing a given situation and playing it out. Rather than going for a theoretical approach to understand how businesses are run and managed, today's managers need to experience the ground realities of running a business and thus internalize the lessons. While Shakespearean plays definitely dwell on fictional constructs, literature is but a reflection of contemporary reality and great literature is a reflection of universal realities to which one need not necessarily put a temporal marker. Hence, Shakespearean plays are of great help in teaching management skills as well. As Peter Brown would tell us about teaching young managers:

> . . . it is not about reading and analyzing a text—it is about playing things out. When Henry tells his troops "we are going to France," he is selling a vision. A modern leader also needs to sell a vision. If s/he uses commitment and passion—the chances are people in the organization will listen more than if one uses a PowerPoint presentation. (Brown: Online)

The management teacher can also contrast *Henry V* with *King Lear* to help today's managers discuss an overconfident leader like Lear and ask them what he should have done to become a more effective leader. A study of *Macbeth* can throw open a discussion on the problems of over-ambitiousness and greed and its impact on human relationships. Macbeth believes that one murder can set things right for him forever but it is this failure to see the consequences of a wrong move that ultimately drowns him in life and death. A manager similarly needs to distinguish between desirable and undesirable steps so as to help the company move ahead in an ethical and integrated manner. In fact, almost all plays of Shakespeare can be effectively put to use to energize and empower management education.

However, this idea does not cut ice with one and all. Some scholars and experts are of the opinion that it is wastage of both literary as well as management resources to bring in Shakespeare to the management classroom. Management critics like Dr. Thomas McGrath find problems with taking up Shakespeare for teaching managerial lessons. He is of the view that this process involves over-simplification of Shakespeare and hence is out of context. To put it in his words:

> There are problems there. . . They are literary constructs. It's impoverishing management and it's impoverishing Shakespeare. . . Shakespeare is taken out of context. These management gurus are looking at the shop floor person, the whistle blower, the fool in King Lear. They've got the answers. (Quoted in Brown: Online)

While one needs to agree with McGrath in that Shakespeare is somewhat simplified for management education, it nevertheless serves the purpose of sensitizing the modern day managers towards human relationships and also trains them on various hands-on managerial skills. To throw in some more examples, *Taming of the Shrew* teaches lessons on change management; *The Merchant of Venice* on risk management and diversity; and *Hamlet* has valuable lessons to offer on crisis management (Williams: Online). Furthermore, the plays can be contextualized with some effort from the teacher-student team and thus a single play can be adapted to teach and learn multiple managerial skills in the classroom situation. Hence, Shakespeare's crucial comprehension of the palace politics can definitely work for understanding the functions of the modern day corporate world.

One can thus conclude that as "business involves people and people fundamentally don't change," Shakespeare has ample lessons to offer to the present day managers (Callahan: Online). While business has now become competent and fast-moving with newer means and modes of technology on offer such as e-mails, telephones, cell phones, the internet, and PCs, the basics of doing and running businesses successfully still depends on human nature. And who better than the Bard can we have to give us an insight into human nature? More importantly, modern day management students still are able to connect to the kings, queens, and lords of Shakespeare and gain newer perspectives on human life in general and business in particular. It is hence apt to conclude that teaching management through Shakespeare is perhaps one of the best ways to keep alive the essence of the plays and also bring them into the modern day management context.

If management is about motivating people to excel and do it in a moving diction then there is nobody better than Shakespeare who has to his credit some of the best dialogues on group communication. Hence, it is in fact very inspiring to teach managers the lessons on running and maintaining businesses through a playful and engrossing study of the Bard's works. By taking the managers to a world very different from the modern world, the teacher can offer them opportunities to expand their perspectives and learn from such experiences. Businesses, as mentioned earlier, are run by people and it is people that Shakespeare talks about. Hence, managers as people can learn a plethora of skills from the plays of Shakespeare and apply them in their day-to-day business practices.

Works Cited

Brown, Peter. "Can Shakespeare really be a useful management tool?" (2007): 4pp. 12 October 2008. <http://www.independent.co.uk/student/postgraduate/mbas-guide/can-shakespeare-really-be-a-useful-management-tool-432519.html>

Bailey, Margery. "Shakespeare in Action." *College English* 15.6 (1954): 307-315.

Callahan, Kathryn. "Executives Turn to Shakespeare." (2000): 3pp. 27 November 2008. <http://www.vault.co.in/nr/newsmain.jsp?nr_page=3&ch_id=402&article_id=51643&cat_id=2071>

Corrigan, Paul. *Shakespeare on Management: Leadership Lessons for Today's Managers*. London: Kogan Page Publishers, 2000.

Hill, Alma Blinn. "Hamlet as an Undergraduate." *College English* 36.1 (1974): 122-125.

Narayanswamy, Ramnath. "Why the Arts are Integral to Management Education?." *Economic and Political Weekly* 36.46/47 (Nov 24-30, 2001): 4358-4368.

Newstorm, John W. "Human Relations Training for Middle Management: Comment." *The Academy of Management Journal* 14.2 (1971): 265-267.

William Shakespeare: The Complete Works. Ed. Wells et al. Oxford: Clarendon Press, 1991.

Williams, Judy. "Lessons of the Bard."(2009): 5pp. 14 February 2009. <http://hre.lrp.com/HRE/story.jsp?storyId=4361962>

7

From Scottish Highlands to Feudal Japan: *Macbeth* and *The Throne of Blood*

— Aysha Viswamohan

The interdisciplinary field of "cultural studies" is less interested in establishing vertical hierarchies of value than in exploring "horizontal" relations between neighbouring media. From a cultural studies perspective, adaptation forms part of a flattened out and newly egalitarian spectrum of cultural productions. Structuralist and post-structuralist theoretical developments subvert many of the prejudices and hierarchies, and thus have an impact on the issues of adaptation. The structuralist semiotics of the nineteen-sixties and seventies treated all signifying practices as shared sign systems productive of "texts" worthy of the same critical readings as literary texts, thus abolishing the hierarchy between novel and film. Bakhtin's attitude toward the literary author as inhabiting "inter-individual territory" suggested a devalourisation of artistic "originality." Despite the perennial comparisons of the artist to a god or creator, the artist's actual role is caught up in more modest, more typically human interactions. As what Bakhtin calls a "hybrid construction," the artistic utterance always mingles one's own word with the other's word. Adaptation, too, can be seen as an orchestration of discourses, talents, and tracks. It is a hybrid construction of different media and discourses.

Coming to the reception theory, a text is an event, whose indeterminacies are completed and actualized in the reading (or spectating). Rather than being merely portrayals of a pre-existing reality, both novel and film are communicative utterances, socially situated and historically shaped. Like poststructuralism, reception theory, too, undermines the notion of a semantic core, a nucleus of meaning, ascribable to novel, which adaptations are presumed to "capture" or "betray." Furthermore, contemporary theory assumes that texts do not know themselves, and therefore seeks out the unsaid of texts. The Postmodern era is one in which reproduction takes over from authentic production. Marxist critics like Terry Eagleton and Fredric Jameson belong to this specific school. For French theorist, Jean Baudrillard, postmodern culture is dominated by the simulacrum or the copy, which has come to replace the "real." T. Jefferson Kline discusses the kinds of intertextuality across the boundaries, especially between film and literature. James Goodwin's study of the films of Kurosawa explores the hybridity of Japanese and Western cultures in the director's films.

Akira Kurosawa

Kurosawa is remembered as a master technician and stylist, with a deep humanism and compassion for his characters and an awe of the enormity of nature. He awakened the West to Japanese cinema with *Rashomon*, which won the top prize in the Venice Film Festival of 1951, and also a special Oscar for best foreign film. Kurosawa's *Seven Samurai* was remade in the US under its alternative title *The Magnificent Seven* and the lone samurai hero Yojimbo was the inspiration for Clint Eastwood's man with no name persona, most obviously in *A Fistful of Dollars*. Most Japanese films fall under two categories: the *jidai-geki* (or period films) and the *gendai-mono* (or modern story). In *Macbeth*, Kurosawa perceived a contemporary theme, namely, a parallel between medieval Scotland and medieval Japan which mirrored contemporary society.

Macbeth and *The Throne of Blood*

The story of *Macbeth* held a special attention for Kurosawa. Based on *Macbeth*, *The Throne of Blood* proves there is much more to Shakespeare's work than the language. Directed, adapted and edited by Kurosawa, the film starred Toshiro Mifune (Washizu/ Macbeth), Isuzu Yamada (Asaji/Lady Macbeth) and Minoru

Chiaki (Miki/Banquo). Though unable to make use of the poetry of the original, Kurosawa carefully preserves the dramatic dynamics and visual vitality of the play. His translation is so complete, the film seems totally Japanese in its character and totally cinematic in its language. The film is set in medieval Japan, during "the Age of the Country at War," a period when feudal Japan was undergoing Civil War (1392-1568). This was a time when violations of the Samurai code were a concern, a time when traitors and renegade samurai were common figures and real kings were deposed in similar circumstances to the Lords in *The Throne of Blood* (*Kumonosu-Djo* in Japanese, literally means "The Castle of the Spider's Web"). It must be noted that the Samurai were a doomed class, disbanded in the nineteenth century. This idea is always present for an audience—along with the knowledge that whatever action the hero chooses, his whole lifestyle is fundamentally doomed. The word "'samurai" is derived from the word *sabarau* meaning "to serve." In *The Throne of Blood* this is ironic, of course, as the whole world of the samurai is shown to be corrupt and self-serving. In place of an individual with a tragic flaw, as Macbeth is, we have a whole society with the tragic flaw of feudalism. To the extent that *The Throne of Blood* is about a trapped individual destroyed by a rigid social structure, the film can be read as an anti-feudal drama.

The famous opening scene of *Macbeth* has three witches chanting magical rhymes, which signal the play's themes of paradox and ambiguity. These utterances also establish an important ritualistic framework for the play. As if to demonstrate the power of witchcraft on Macbeth, Macbeth tells Banquo, "So foul and fair a day I have not seen."

The film, *The Throne of Blood,* however starts with an elegiac note. At the beginning, says the chorus:

> Once stood a mighty fortress where
> Lived a proud warrior
> Murdered by ambition
> His spirit walking still.

The final chorus, at the end of the film, repeats the story and reinforces the moral:

Still his spirit walks, his fame is known,
For what once was is now yet true,
Murderous ambition will pursue.

The story begins as General Washizu and his friend, General Miki, lose their way in a forest, as they return after quashing a rebellion against the king. In the forest, they meet a witch who prophesies that Washizu will reign but Miki's descendents will inherit the land. Visually, the film tries to capture the good and evil side of human nature. Photographed in stark black and white, everything is either-or. It must be noticed that Washizu's banner carries the totemic emblem of a centipede, while the flag of Miki bears a rabbit. The film begins and ends with the same image, including stony paths, the ruins of a castle and drifting fog. In fact, Kurosawa uses the all-pervasive imagery of fog, labyrinths and boundaries throughout. From the outset, Kurosawa suggests that there is no freedom, no escape where an aura of uncertainty looms large. In the opening scene, Washizu and Miki ride in and out of fog no less than twelve times.

Plot

While drawing from Shakespeare, Kurosawa lends his distinct touches to the proceedings. Every action, for instance, mirrors a parallel. The original rebel, from whom Washizu defended the lord, becomes Washizu himself. The dead lord's lady kills herself as does Asaji who commits suicide. After Miki/Banquo's murder, during the banquet the *kyogen* dancer/singer says:

All of you wicked. Listen while
I tell of a man, vain,
Sinful, vile–
Who, though ambitious, insolent
Could not escape his punishment.

The song becomes a comment. The past warriors had the same career as Washizu, and he will end the way they have, guilty of *ge-koku-jo* (regicide). Kurosawa thus implies inevitability, yet mindless repetition of destiny. Washizu/ Macbeth's death is far from heroic. By the end, Asaji has miscarried and died and

Washizu has lost his precious sleep. The rebels surround the castle and Washizu's servants speak of the rats abandoning the castle. As Washizu addresses his War Council, suddenly the rooms are invaded by birds. While the lord's men gape in astonishment at the trapped birds swooping overhead, the distant sound of wood being cut is heard. The rebels are destroying the forest, a clever allusion to Birnam Wood of the original.

Washizu has immense faith in the forest. "No one could defeat the man who planned this place. They cannot see us here inside, while we can see them all." No wonder he stands confounded as the wood advances upon him, while he leans from the ramparts of his castle. The magical forest is powerless to save him now. Washizu panics and then is pumped with arrows shot by samurai. (Viewers may note the conspicuous omission of Macduff and his wife and children). For Kurosawa, Washizu is as much a victim of a constraining feudal order and social decorum as of his personal sins.

Noh Traditions in *The Throne of Blood*

The world of the Noh is both closed and artificial, and is widely referred to throughout the film. Begun around the twelfth century, the Noh theatre emerged as a highly esoteric presentational form which relies on dance, music, masks, and declamatory narrative to relate traditional folk tales. In Noh, one decodes the gestures, the masks, the music, and not the narrative being related. Its degree of compression is extreme, and it is full of symbols. Kurosawa preferred Noh to any other Japanese art form since, according to him, it was the core of all Japanese drama. In adherence to the tradition, the director avoids close-up shots of his characters because in Noh everything is seen full. This further leads to building an alienation effect.

An interesting aspect of the film is that the Noh elements are mostly associated with Asaji, the Lady Macbeth role, for she is the most limited, and most evil. Her body language, her hand washing and her scenes with Washizu are most Noh-like. Other Noh aspect is the role of the witch. Her reed hut is akin to a Noh set and so is her make up. Her prophecies are articulated in the husky and unintonated voice of the Noh actor, and the sounds which both women make, that is, the squeak of Asaji's *tabi* (the traditional socks), the sound of her *kimono*, the clatter of the witch's spinning wheel, are sounds one would associate with the Noh. It appears that the two women are the movers of the plot, and in Kurosawa (as in Shakespeare), women are truly on the side of evil. Indeed, as Asaji says at one point, "This is a wicked world. To save yourself you often first must kill. . . . Children kill their parents for less" (cf. Macbeth: "Come you spirits/That tend on mortal thoughts, unsex me here/ And fill me from the crown to the toe, top-full/ Of direst cruelty"). This is ironic; as it is her own child who is still-born causes her death. Asaji's ideas are on par with the witch's who proclaims, "If you choose ambition, then choose it honestly, with cruelty. . . . If you would make a mountain of the dead, then pile it to the sky; if you should shed blood, then let it run as a river." Again, when Washizu expresses disbelief at her prophecy, the witch retorts, "You humans! Never will I comprehend you. . . . You are afraid of your desires. You attempt to hide them." One gets a feeling she and Asaji would have understood each other well.

Unlike Wahizu, Asaji is portrayed as a person who knows her mind. She knows what she wants and if Miki gets in her way, then he must be removed. Her rigidity is closer to Noh than anything else in the film. This is a far cry from Washizu who is too afraid and too much divided. No wonder Asaji taunts him with, "You who would rule a kingdom are yet afraid of a ghost." This is akin to her earlier rebuke, "Without ambition, man is not a man." However, Kurosawa's concern is starkly different and operates on a metaphysical level. He agonizes, "Why is it that human beings cannot get along with each other?"

Conclusion

Both *Macbeth* and *The Throne of Blood* can be seen primarily as social tragedies set within a distanced historical context in which social problems and contradictions can be rendered visible to the spectators. *The Throne of Blood* is a rich text that benefits from a viewing that includes knowledge of *Macbeth,* as much as it is enriched by familiarity with Japanese culture. It is new and yet timeless, largely due to the fusion of its two main sources and cultures: Shakespeare's English play and Japanese Noh theatre. Like the *doubloon* (literally, a pure gold coin) in *Moby Dick* which lends itself to multiple readings and analyses by a motley group of sailors, so do various works of Shakespeare, and Kurosawa's *Macbeth* is a prime example of this trend.

Notes

Some acclaimed adaptations of Shakespeare are as follows. The list is not definitive by any means:

a) Kurosawa's *Ran (King Lear)*
b) Orson Welles's *Macbeth*
c) Franco Zeffirelli's *The Taming of the Shrew*
d) Jean-Luc Godard's *King Lear*
e) Peter Brooks's *King Lear*
f) Gulzar's *Angoor* (*Comedy of Errors*)
g) Jane Smiley's *A Thousand Acres* (*King Lear*) turned into film
h) *Hamlet 2000*, a modern day adaptation of *Hamlet*
i) Vishal Bhardwaj's *Maqbool* (*Macbeth*) and *Omkara* (*Othello*)
j) *Kiss me Kate* and *10 Things I Hate About You*, adaptation of *Taming of the Shrew*.

Works Cited

Allen, Graham. *Intertextuality*. London & New York: Routledge, 2007.

Davies, Anthony. *Filming Shakespeare's Plays*. Cambridge: Cambridge University Press, 1988.

Dollimore, Jonathan and Alan Sinfield (eds). *Political Shakespeare*. Manchester: Manchester University Press, 1985.

Goodwin, James. *Akira Kurosawa and Intertextual Cinema*. Baltimore: John Hopkins University Press, 1994.

Kline, T. J. *Screening the Text*. Baltimore: Johns Hopkins University Press, 1992.

Hindle, Maurice. *Studying Shakespeare on Film*. New York: Palgrave Macmillan, 2007.

Holderness, Graham. *Shakespeare Recycled: The Making of Historical Drama*. Hertfordshire: Harvester Wheatsheaf, 1992.

______________ . "Radical Potentiality and Institutional Closure." *Shakespeare: Macbeth*. Ed. John Wain. London: Macmillan, 1968.

Richie, Donald. *The Films of Akira Kurosawa*. Berkeley: University of California Press, 1998.

Stam, Robert and Alessandra Raengo. *Literature and Film*. MA: Blackwell, 2005.

8

Imprint of Shakespeare on the Indian Stage and Screen

— T. Asha Priya and M. G. Priya

> Drama is an art in which the written word of the playwright attains complete artistic realization only when it becomes the spoken word of the actor on the stage and through that medium reacts on the minds of the audience (M. K. Naik 29).

Drama is complicated by the need to give attention to the several stages in its making: its writing by the playwright, the text or script of the play, its production and performance, and the audience for whom it is intended. It should be studied not in parts but as a whole; it should be synthesized and not analyzed. Both the play and the performance have three living, shifting relationships—the script, the author and the audience. So, a student/critic of drama is concerned with the script's anticipation, author's preference, the quality of the actors' interpretation of the signals and their reception by the audience.

J.B. Priestley once said that true drama is created by bringing life to the theatre and the theatre to life. True to the Priestleyan sense, Shakespeare's plays have stood the test of time and have been performed at different stages all over the world. The production of Shakespeare's plays began in India in "Garrison theatres" which catered to British colonists. There have been many performances of Shakespeare's plays whether in their original form, stage adaptations or cinematic adaptations.

Shakespeare in the Indian Screen

World over, Shakespeare has been given credit in six hundred and forty two films. Indian cinema has been borrowing from Shakespeare for about a century. Shakespeare was first adapted in India in the 1928 film, *Khoon-e-Nakak* (Murder Most Foul). This was a silent film based on *Hamlet* made by the actor turned director K.B. Athavale. Film historian Firoze Rangoonwalla recalls that *Dilfarosh*, a 1930s film, was based on *The Merchant of Venice.* Shades of *The Tempest* can be seen in the 1930s costume drama *Aab-e-Hayat*. And parts of *Aan* (starring Dilip Kumar and Nadira), *Ziddi* (Asha Parekh and Joy Mukherjee), *Dharamveer* (Dharmendra and Zeenat Aman), *Betaab* (Sunny Deol and Amrita Singh) are inspired by *The Taming of the Shrew*.

Ashish Rajadhyaksha, in the *Encyclopaedia of Indian Cinema*, credits Sohrab Modi with bringing "Shakespeare to the Indian screen." The reason why everybody in the cinema and theatre fraternity has borrowed from Shakespeare the Bard is perhaps because each director has felt that Shakespeare can be located in a very Indian context. Purshottam Nedungadi, scholar-author from Calicut in Kerala, has said in a lighter vein, "Do not be intimidated by Shakespeare. He is one of us. He is basically, a *moplah* from North Kerala who is called, Sheikh Speare!"

Apart from straight adaptations, Shakespeare has inspired countless Hindi films. Traces of *Romeo and Juliet* theme have been seen in films like *Qayamat Se Qayamat Tak, Maine Pyaar Kiya; The Comedy of Errors* motif has been used in movies like Jayant Desai's *Bhool Bhulaiyan* in 1933, the Gulzaar written and Bimal Roy produced *Do Dooni Chaar*, and Gulzaar's own adaptation *Angoor*, starring Sanjeev Kumar and Deven Verma. Gulzaar remodelled *The Comedy of Errors* in his *Angoor* toning it to the Indian socio-cultural environment and it was a masterpiece. A feel of *Hamlet* can be felt in the movie *Karz*. Shakespeare's comedies like *Twelfth Night* in which Viola dresses up as a man in order to "find her love" is almost a familiar feature in our films. The Indian films with "royal kings and queens" story in them have been highly influenced by *King Lear* wherein we see how the king is usually unaware of the real love and is "falsely impressed by people who flatter him." Shakespeare, then, is very much in the Indian heritage.

Vishal Bharadwaj's *Omkara* brought Shakespeare and Othello right into the mindscape of the mainstream Indian Cinema.

Omkara, based on *Othello,* is only the latest in the long line of Indian films that have drawn from Shakespeare's plays. *Omkara* is set in Uttar Pradesh. It is a tragic love story that stars big Bollywood names like Naseeruddin Shah, Ajay Devgan and Kareena Kapoor. National award winner Ajay Devgan plays the lead role in *Omkara,* a short-tempered lover, whose jealousy destroys his happiness and love. Though Devgan plays the role of an outlaw chief, *Omkara* is not an action movie, but rather dwells on the complexity of human relationships, as any Shakespearean play does. *Omkara* is beautifully made and powerful, but lacks something in its interpretation of the character. This adaptation portrays how Shakespeare transcends time and place. His plays can be recreated in any form. Bharadwaj also recast *Macbeth* and adapted it to *Maqbool.*

In Tamil, Pammal Sambandam Mudaliar drew inspiration from many Shakespearean works. He wrote *Vaanipurathu Vanigan,* the Tamil version of *The Merchant of Venice.* There was even a Tamil film called *Shylock* (1940) made by Serukalathur Sama who wrote, directed and played the title role in it. He retained the Shakespearean names for all the characters and even costumes were designed very similar to those used by the Elizabethan artistes. Unfortunately, the audience did not appreciate this film and the screenplay of the movie was sold at one *anna* (an *anna* is one-sixteenth of a rupee). Noted filmmaker K.V. Reddy adapted the Shakespearean tragedy *King Lear* in Telugu and gave it a folklore format in *Gunasundari Katha.* It was a roaring success and was later made in Tamil also.

Several films have been and are being adapted from Shakespeare's various plays and the *desi* twist to Shakespeare has found favour with the Indian audience and has evoked wide appreciation.

Shakespeare in the Indian Stage

India has a rich theatrical tradition with the vital convergence of the past and the present, the physical and the verbal, the sacred and the profane, the comic and the tragic, the magic and the real. India, despite being a large sub-continent with a lot of cultural and regional differences, has whole-heartedly accepted Shakespeare. Localizing Shakespeare has never been a problem in India since

Shakespearean characters are universal transcending the boundaries of time and place.

H.S. Sivaprakash says that translation is an act of transfer of knowledge, information and ideas from one language to another; it is a colonial enterprise and it implies certain relationship of power among the languages and cultures involved. Many of the translations of Shakespeare were adaptations meant to introduce Shakespeare to ordinary Indians. They displayed different levels of localization—from a simple Indianization of names and images, to a re-location in a specified period of time and history, to a retelling with the addition and removal of characters, scenes and subplots along with the interpolation of songs and dances—a total Indianization of a traditional western theatre form.

The year 1852 saw the recognizable translation of *The Merchant of Venice* in Bengali and the first performance of *The Taming of the Shrew* in Gujarati at the Andrews Library in Surat. A Shakespeare theatrical company is known to have been established in 1876 with the purpose of presenting Shakespeare's plays in Gujarati in translation, but with Elizabethan costumes. The number of translations of Shakespeare's plays was more in the end of the nineteenth century, but these were designed more for study than for performance, like the Sanskrit version of *Dream* by R. Krishnamacharya.

Later, after independence, Indians became versatile and Shakespeare was placed at a still higher pedestal. At this stage, there were serious attempts in translating the poetry and stageability of Shakespeare's plays. Trivedi has pointed out the three-fold process of development:

i) Conscious universalization of Shakespeare without any Indianness;
ii) Assimilating Shakespeare into the traditional performance and the philosophic fabric of India, like B.V. Karanth's *Macbeth* performed in *Yakshagana,* a Kannada folk play;
iii) Rewriting the Shakespearean text in the contemporary lingo like Roysten Abel's bilingual *Othello: A Play in Black and White.*

O' Lear was one of the five best plays of a total of twenty-one plays staged at the Eleventh National Drama Festival held at the Nehru

Centre in Mumbai. In this Mysore based Rangayana Theatre's adaptation of the play, Chidambara Rao Jambe, the director, has remained largely faithful to the original script but has more pertinently changed the ending. The happy end marks a departure from the original tragedy in which both Lear and Cordelia die. This end is however not in contradiction with the layers of interpretation that the production brings about. One can perceive the director's touch as the play raises questions about life, ageing, relationships and insecurity. It is complete in its ability to rise above time and becomes more like a circle that has no beginning, middle or end.

The set design is simplified giving rise to the endless possibilities of dramatic compositions and unobtrusive fluidity to the movements of the actors. The space is almost neutral with an irregular mound in the centre that occupied a large area. At the stage right a high platform had a covered front while at the stage left, a sort of insignia suspended from the top. It was dimly lit by a rectangular jute piece with bright red or a blue-coloured spotlight falling in between. This set would perhaps have not been so effective were it not for the imaginative use of lights. Throughout the play the lighting sustains a chiaroscuro quality and reveals only as much as is needed. Along with dark and light shades the use of primary colours was bold and effective. No action was missed in the dark and nothing was unnecessarily illuminated. The muted and the unsophisticated dark robe of Lear created an image of an animal caged in his past, a giant bird unable to take off. The daughters were adequately dressed and so were the jesters and the courtiers.

The set design and the stage property at hand were innovative and some of the touches were brilliant. For instance, the scene in which the demented king thrashes the two puppets, which symbolized his two elder daughters, was so evocative that even without knowing a word, the act touches the heart. The most significant contribution to the success of the show was the team of actors. From Lear to the smallest role-player, the artists displayed much conviction in the script and in the characters they assumed. From Lear to jester, from the princesses to the servants and the messengers, each role was wholesome.

Credit for this wonderful production goes to H.S. Shivaprakash for translating the play into Kannada, to

Chidambara Rao Jambe for direction, H.K. Dwarakanath for stage design, Sagai Raju for illumunation, Mahadeva for operating the lights, to Saroja Hegde/Srinivas Bhat for their music and finally to Santosh Kumar Kasanoor for his brilliant performance as King Lear.

Shakespeare lends himself superbly to adaptations unlike many other European playwrights. In a production of *Hamlet* by Pravah Theatre Laboratory, directed by Neeraj Kabi, Yakshagana dancers acted out the play within the play, to the accompaniment of Dhrupad music. Gertrude wore an *odhni* (shawl) lined in red and *sindoor* in her *maang* (parting of the hair). And, her dialogues were in pure Hindi, translated by Harivansh Rai Bachchan. The packed house reacted with surprise and awe, a reaction that Kabi is by now familiar with, having performed in Mumbai and Delhi at the National School of Drama Festival. For Kabi, *Hamlet* was only the beginning; it continued with *Macbeth* in 2007; and later a series of other Shakespearean plays.

The ability to find truth in stylization, life in the rituals and beauty and form in spontaneity are all abilities that bound and this enriches the playing of Shakespeare's plays. In the cast, we have dancers, modern realistic actors, musicians, street artists, and performers trained in theatrical forms two thousand years old, and others who have taken these forms and adapted them into new forms. This is the natural make-up of a group of Indian performers of Shakespeare.

Playpen, a theatre group managed by Mahesh Dattani put up several plays of Shakespeare, the memorable one being *The Tempest*. Mahesh Dattani, in an interview with Riti, said, "William Shakespeare is as much the heritage of the Indians as the British. . . . We are trying to bring out its true relevance to twentieth century India." This is a cross-cultural interpretation where Prospero wears dhoti and the other characters look as if they have just come out of the Indian folk theatre. This was directed by Michael Walling who has directed Shakespearean drama in the US and the UK. Riti adds, "Dattani and Walling feel that *The Tempest* is particularly relevant to a country experiencing the aftermath of colonization as its theme deals with the conflict between the natural inhabitants and the intruders" (quoted in Lindsay Pereira: Online).

One of the three reasons for Shakespeare's plays being adapted in the regional languages and cultures is the delight of travelling from one literary tradition to another discovering that the boundaries are porous; another is the delight of translating from a global world language to another language; the third reason is the freedom that the directors get to reconstruct and modify the stage directions as Shakespeare gives only expressive instructions. Thus, by giving Shakespeare a *desi* twist, the old colonization is transformed into globalization.

Shakespeare has other formative effects on the structure, themes and literary aspects of modern Indian drama. A new model of poetic drama combined with the classical Indian model on one hand, and various popular and folk models on the other, came into existence. Shakespeare's dramatics, combined with the traditions of classical Indian drama as well as popular folk theatre, formed a beautiful cocktail to relish the Indian audience. Such hybrid Shakespeare can be seen in almost all the parts of India starting with the Jatra in Bengal, the Nautanki in Northern India and the Yakshagana and Kathakali in the south. In 1996, artistes from the International Centre staged Sadanan Balakrishnan's adapted version of *Othello* in Kathakali form. The dramatization retained the traditional grammar; the *padams* were in *manipravalam* and the musical style in *Sopanam*. The play had a larger-than-life representation in Kathakali. It was enacted in the very traditional manner in front of the flickering flames of a brass lamp, with the typical *thirasheela* (curtain) used for dramatic effects. The whole enactment captured the strong passions of the characters.

The Indian-Australian-French Annette Leday/Keli Company performed

King Lear in the Kathakali mode, at the reconstruction of Shakespeare's Globe Theatre on the Thames between sixth and seventeenth of July 1999 as part of the Annual Globe Festival, which features international productions of the bard's work. This interculturalism in the history of Shakespearean theatre, writes Rustom Bharucha, "evokes a back-and-forth movement, suggesting the swing of the pendulum" (quoted in Halliburton: Online). The viewers of this powerful combination of Shakespeare and Kathakali, no doubt, got an excellent taste of both art forms and could enjoy the conventionalized registering of *bhavas* (emotions) on the performers' countenance. Shakespeare scholar, Richard Hornbey, for example, found the final scene "as poignant as I have ever seen it, although both actors were so covered in gilt, jewels, head dresses, robes and thick make-up as to resemble porcelain dolls" (quoted in Diane 88)

This performance at the Globe is incidentally a case study in the possibilities and the difficulties of intercultural theatre practice. This production by a multinational troupe collaborating over ten years crafted a work that transcends Indian and European cultural boundaries. It stands testimony to the fact as to how art is beyond boundaries. The fusion of western theatre with the physicalisation of emotions by Kathakali masters brought out a new experience for the audience to experience Lear and Kathakali anew, providing a positive model for further intercultural work.

Postcolonial dramatists take the middle path between the parrot like repetition of an English Shakespeare and the complete rejection of Shakespeare—the fashionable notion of the "hybrid performance". The Hybrid Shakespeare contains elements of both cultures—the British as well as the host culture—in such a manner that the combination sheds light on both the cultures. Ania Loomba calls the Kathakali version of *Othello* as an example of post-colonial hybrid Shakespeare. This hybrid variety recognizes both the differences as well as similarities between the English Renaissance and the local present. The advent of hybrid Shakespeare "provincialized Shakespeare" and the confluence of Shakespeare's dramatics and the present day Indian local dramatics makes Shakespeare's plays very much relevant.

The past two decades have witnessed an array of new approaches to Shakespeare on screen ranging from Peter Greenway's genre-binding experiments in "database" cinema to Michael Almereyadas's recasting of Hamlet as a devotee of visual technologies as well as to Julia Taymor's postmodern collisions of time and space. It is in the performance of Shakespeare on Indian stages in Indian theatrical forms rather than in the classroom that the response of India to Shakespeare can be seen. Consequently, Shakespeare studies now have diversified to include many areas like performance studies, film studies, cultural and intercultural studies, translations and postcolonial studies.

Works Cited

Chaudhuri, Sukanta. "Shakespeare in India." 25 Feb. 2009. <http://internet shakespeare.uvic.ca/library/criticism/shakespeare inindia1.html>

Diane, Daugherty. "The Pendulum of Intercultural Performance: *Kathakali King Lear* at Shakespeare's Globe." *Asian Theatre Journal* 22.1 (Spring 2005): 87-92.

Halliburton, Rachel. "Theatre: India Plays England at the Globe: A Kathakali Company is staging *King Lear*." 7 July 1999. <http://www.independent.co.uk/arts-entertainment/theatre-india-plays-england-at-the-globe-1104785>.

Loomba, Ania and Martin Orkin. *Post-Colonial Shakespeares*. London: Routledge, 1998.

Naik, M.K. *Dimensions of Indian English Literature*. New Delhi: Sterling Publishers, 1987.

Pereira, Lindsay. "William Shakespeare is our Heritage Too." 26 September 2006. <http://www.rediff.com///news/2006/sep/26inter.html>

Ravindran, Nirmala. "The Bard is Back." 24 January 2009. <http://archives.digitaltoday.in/indiatoday/20060410/society2.html>

Trivedi, Poonam and Dennis Bartholomeusz. *India's Shakespeare: Translation, Interpretation, and Performance*. Delaware, US: University of Delaware Press, 2005.

9

The Force in Shakespeare's Plays in Sri Aurobindo's Perspective

— Shruti Bidwaikar

For five çenturies Shakespeare has occupied the academia and has unceasingly invited new interpretations and insights on his plays. Since the time he wrote, many eminent poets and critics have found something of interest to them in Shakespeare. With such varied interests, parameters and insights, they have come up with startling interpretations of Shakespeare's plays. Today, insights from gender studies, psychoanalytical theories, and theories on archetypes, deconstruction, reader-response criticism and post-colonial studies are being applied to his plays in various degrees and dimensions.

Sri Aurobindo, a poet and a critic, has written commentaries on Shakespeare's plays, although there is no theorizing on his part. He has approached the plays on the plane on which they worked. He calls it "the life-plane" or "the vital plane." Sri Aurobindo observes: "Shakespeare was the poet of life seen through an identity of feeling with it and of thought arising out of the surge of life" (*Sri Aurobindo on Shakespeare* 69). This is implied in what Sri Aurobindo calls the "five suns of poetry", which are "Truth, Beauty, Delight, Life and Spirit" (*The Future Poetry* 222). Linking all these terms he says: "The enlightening power of the poet's creation is vision of truth, its moving power is a passion of beauty and delight, but its sustaining power and that which makes it great and vital is the breath of life" (*The Future Poetry* 242).

According to Sri Aurobindo, Shakespeare expressed the vital plane most powerfully in his plays. His major characters have the vigour, force, desire, ambition, will-power and such impulses which direct their lives. His characters philosophize on life essentially making sense of the human existence. It is this life plane which strikes the reader; life in its best and worst. Thought is very much there, but the action is based essentially on the level of existence and thought works for the sake of life. This article aims to study Shakespeare applying Sri Aurobindo's "vital plane" design to *Macbeth*.

Sri Aurobindo observes, "In all very great drama the movement and result is really psychological and the outward action, even when it is considerable, and the consummating event, even though loud and violent, are only either its symbol or else its condition of culmination" (*Sri Aurobindo on Shakespeare* 63). A.C. Bradley propounds a similar thought: "The 'story' or action of a Shakespearean tragedy does not consist, of course, solely of human actions or deeds; but the deeds are the predominant factor. And these deeds are for the most part, actions in the full sense of the word; not things done 'tween asleep and wake', but acts or omissions thoroughly expressive of the doer, characteristic deeds. The centre of the tragedy, therefore, may be said, with equal truth, to lie in action issuing from character, or in character issuing in action" (7).

This psychology of drama or expression of the doer is exemplified clearly in Macbeth's fantasy of the dagger, where he sees the dagger dangling before him and fails to catch hold of it:

> Is this a dagger which I see before me,
> The handle toward my hand? Come, let me clutch thee.
> I have thee not, and yet I see thee still.
> Art thou not, fatal vision, sensible
> To feeling as to sight? Or art thou but
> A dagger of the mind, a false creation,
> Proceeding from the heat-oppressed brain? (2. 1. 33-39)

Yet another such reaction is at the sight of the Ghost of Banquo. Macbeth is overwhelmed with fear and his conscience pricks him for having committed two murders:

> Avaunt! And quit my sight! Let the earth hide thee!
> Thy bones are marrowless, thy blood is cold;

> Thou has no speculation in those eyes
> Which thou dost glare with! (3. 4. 93-96)

Sri Aurobindo says, "... the combination of words and sounds in Shakespeare's line, so arranged as to force on the mind and still more on the subtle nerves and sense the utter absoluteness of the difficulty and pain of living for the soul that has awakened to the misery of the world" (*Sri Aurobindo on Shakespeare* 17). Macbeth's condition as revealed in the soliloquy after he murders Duncan is one example of such a fix:

> But wherefore could not I pronounce 'Amen'?
> I had most need of Blessing, and 'Amen'
> Stuck my throat. (2. 2. 31-33)

Then,

> Methought I heard a voice cry 'Sleep no more!
> Macbeth does murder sleep',—the innocent sleep,
> Sleep that knits up the ravell'd sleeve of care,
> The death of each day's life, sore labour's bath,
> *Balm* of hurt minds, great nature's second course,
> Chief nourisher in life's feast.
> Still it cried 'Sleep no more!' to all the house:
> 'Glamis hath murder'd sleep, and therefore Cawdor
> Shall sleep no more; Macbeth shall sleep no more.'
> (2. 2. 35-43)

Then,

> Whence is that knocking?
> How is't with me, when every noise appals me?
> What hands are here? ha! They pluck out mine eyes.
> Will all great Neptune's Ocean wash this blood
> Clean from my hand? No, this my hand will rather
> The multitudinous seas incarnadine,
> Making the green one red. (2. 2. 57-63)

Lady Macbeth's confession during her ailment has a similar quandary:

> What need we fear who knows it, when none can call our power to account? Yet who would have thought the old man to have had so much blood in him. (5. 1. 44-48)

> Here's the smell of the blood still: all the perfumes of Arabia will not sweeten this little hand. Oh, oh, oh! (5. 1. 55-57)
>
> . . . What's done cannot be undone. (5. 1. 75)

In these instances Macbeth and Lady Macbeth are aware of the crime they have committed. They have a troubled conscience and cannot get out of this guilt. Macbeth is stolen of his sleep and peace of mind. Lady Macbeth cannot wake up and rest. The sin/horrors of killing have engulfed them so much that they are not able to come out of their hallucinations. Their souls are awakened to the fact that they have committed the horrendous act, but their minds and lives are unable to bear the burden. This is where Sri Aurobindo's remark "pain of living for the soul that has awakened to the misery of the world" almost becomes nerve-wracking for the two.

Shakespeare's characters come out with a startling understanding of life. Sri Aurobindo calls it the "interpretative vision". He says, "Dramatic poetry" must have "as the fount of its creation or in its heart an interpretative vision and in that vision an explicit or implicit idea of life and the human being"... "This interpretative vision and idea have in the presentation arisen out of the inner life of vital types of the human soul or individual representatives of it." Macbeth's speech after Lady Macbeth's death is a realization that dawn upon him. He says:

> Out, out brief candle!
> Life's but a walking shadow, a poor player
> That struts and frets his hour upon the stage,
> And then is heard no more: it is a tale
> Told by an idiot, full of sound and fury,
> Signifying nothing. (5. 5. 23-28)

And Lady Macbeth's confession "What's done cannot be undone" are words which come out of the inner life of these human beings who have suffered because of their ambitions and vital impulsions.

In the light of Sri Aurobindo's vision, K.D. Sethna analyses the presence of occult forces in the play. The evil deeds done by Macbeth and Lady Macbeth are balanced by the extreme nature of their maladies. Sethna says that both the characters are sensitive and kind and so Macbeth finds the sleeping king "like a new born babe" and Lady Macbeth's awareness of "how tender it is to love the babe that milks one" (*Talks on Poetry* 434) portrays her kindness. In the somnambulist state Lady Macbeth utters, "Who could have thought the old man to have had so much of blood in him?" and her reference to the perfumes of Arabia not being able to wash the smell of blood from her hands are indications of her sensitiveness. However, evil prevails over all that is kind and good in them. They are guided by their ambition. Their suffering is in proportion to the evil they do. Sethna observes:

> Lady Macbeth who goes to the limit of wickedness with hardly a care in the world is the greater sufferer because we must remember how the forces which are occult are also retributive forces; they can avenge an evil action which has been caused by an intervention of evil occult forces, and it is they who rob Macbeth of his sleep and it is they who make Lady Macbeth a sleepwalker, the very opposite of Macbeth. Macbeth, poor fellow, had to pace up and down because he couldn't sleep: he is very restless. She had to pace up and down because she couldn't wake up and rest! So these are sort of balances and the retribution is according to the amount of evil resolution in either (435).

Another point that needs to be mentioned here is about Shakespeare's delineation of minor characters. Sri Aurobindo says: "To the artist nothing is small; he bestows as much of his art within the narrow limits of his small characters as within the wide compass of his greatest. Shakespeare lavishes life upon his minor characters; but in Shakespeare it is the result of an abounding creative energy; he makes living men as God made the world, because he could not help it, because it was in his nature and must out" (*Sri Aurobindo on Shakespeare* 44). For example, Shakespeare putting the words of wisdom in Banquo's mouth:

> That trusted home,
> Might yet enkindle you unto the crown,
> Besides the thane of Cawdor. But 'tis strange:
> And oftentimes, to win us to our harm,
> The instruments of darkness tell us truths,

Win us with honest trifles, to betray us
In deepest consequence. (1. 3. 120-126)

Shakespeare endows Macduff with the heart where he wants to avenge his wife's and children's death:

Tyrant, show thy face!
If thou be'st slain and with no stroke of mine,
My wife and children's ghosts will haunt me still.
I cannot strike at wretched kerns, whose arms
Are hired to bear their staves: either thou, Macbeth,
Or else my sword with an unbatter'd edge,
I sheathe again undeeded. There thou shouldst be;
By this great clatter, one of greatest note
Seems bruited.—Let me find him, fortune!
And more I beg not. (5. 6. 14-23)

I have no words;
My voice is my sword: thou bloodier villain
Than terms can give thee out! (5. 7. 6-8)

It is not only Macbeth who has ambition and remorse and realization of what he does, but other characters are equally imbued with human emotions and feelings, may it be the doctor or the messenger. They have been given the speech which is appropriate to their role and position in the play.

With this revelation it can be concluded that Sri Aurobindo has added a dimension to Shakespeare scholarship with his discussion of the plane on which Shakespeare's plays work. Indeed he takes into account the merits of Shakespeare's language, the impact of the age he lived in, his individual genius and his visionary qualities. In addition, Shakespeare is able to give the interpretative vision of life. Sri Aurobindo says: "Shakespeare was a supreme poet, one might almost say, nothing else" (*Sri Aurobindo on Shakespeare* 9). It is because "Vision is the characteristic power of the poet" writes Sri Aurobindo in *The Future Poetry* (31). It is here that he refers to the ancient idea of Kavi as being the seer-poet. It is not merely for Shakespeare's poetic style that he calls him a poet, but also for his visionary perception.

Works Cited

Bradley, A.C. *Shakespearean Tragedy*. London: Macmillan, 1965.

Sethna, K.D. *Talks on Poetry*. Pondicherry: Sri Aurobindo International Centre of Education, 1989.

______________ . *Sri Aurobindo on Shakespeare*. Pondicherry: Sri Aurobindo Ashram Press, 1991.

Shakespeare, William. *Macbeth*. In *Tragedy*. New Delhi: Classic Paperbacks, 2004: 348-403.

Sri Aurobindo. *The Future Poetry*. Pondicherry: Sri Aurobindo Ashram Press, 1997.

10

Shakespeare's Voice in Gloria Naylor's *Mama Day*

— T. Deivasigamani

Gloria Naylor's novels are punctuated by a set of internal cross-references to characters and places in Shakespeare's works. The range and depth of Shakespearean allusions are particularly significant in Naylor's novel *Mama Day*. In this novel, Naylor's involvement and negotiations with Shakespeare occur in an intermediate zone that conveys a delicate tension in Naylor's perspective on Shakespeare. She appreciates Shakespeare while at the same time she is determined critically to rewrite him. In her review of *Mama Day*, Bharathi Mukerjee praises Naylor's ambitious ability to make the wondrous familiar, but concludes that she fails to establish convincing ties between the love story and issues of large public concern. She notes Naylor's references to *The Tempest* and to slave narratives. Characterized by an excess of plots and characters, *Mama Day* drives its power primarily from the magnificent portrait of the title characters ("There Are Four Sides to Everything" 7).

Naylor's *Mama Day* is a mythical love story that alludes to Shakespeare's *The Tempest*. Her experimentation with voice in *Mama Day* represents a dramatic advance in her artistic talent over her works. Henry Louis Gates states that Naylor achieves in *Mama Day* a "Speaking Text"—one that would seem primarily to be oriented towards imitating one of the numerous forms of oral narration to be found in classical Afro-American vernacular literature" (181). Mama Day's voice serves as spiritual ballast in the narrative, a guide to elemental truths that the other characters must discover to set themselves free. Normally, one would smile at the arbitrary recycling of these incidents and accidents, hints and allegations towards the older work, but in the case of such a successful reinterpretation one might be forgiven for not realizing that props which are completely integrated in the action are also allusions.

Naylor's *Mama Day*, is Shakespearean strand, the interplay between *The Tempest* and Naylor's representation of the Southern island of Willow Springs, involves much more active encounter with Shakespeare. Naylor rewrites the exchange between Prospero and Caliban concerning ownership, in effect honouring Caliban's accusation—"This island's mine, by Sycorax my mother/Which thou tak'st from me"— and reinstating his legitimate, female-derived possession. The black islanders of Willow Springs oppose the trend in island development that would reduce them to Caliban.

Naylor's depiction of Willow Springs' resistance to white corporate and cultural control parallels her own resistance to Shakespearean colonization of her art. However, although Naylor teasingly alludes to Caliban, "some slave on a Caribbean island" Cocoa recalls "from her high school Shakespeare," the main line of Naylor's resistance lies elsewhere. As a recent survey shows, twentieth century attempts to revise *The Tempest* have concentrated on reversing the Prospero-Caliban relationship by imagining a newly empowered Caliban. Naylor's special contribution is focus on women characters, a focus that adds a reconfiguration of genders to the issues of race and class associated with Caliban.

Naylor not only has Mama Day usurp Prospero's role but also redefines that role by altering the prerogatives that go with it. The moral structure of *The Tempest* is carried over into *Mama Day* only in a residual way. For example, Ruby is a Sycorax figure against whom Mama Day is allowed a spectacular punitive display. However, Naylor's main stress is on the differences between Prospero's and Mama Day's magical powers. The storm at the outset of *The Tempest* is Prospero's concoction, as he reveals with paternal reassurance and pride in Act 1 Scene 2. By contrast, Mama Day is powerless to prevent the storm's destruction of Little Caesar, the child whom she had helped Bernice to produce. As Mama Day reflects, "she ain't never tried to get over nature."

While Prospero may belatedly accept the limits of his magic, Mama Day is mindful of her limitations from the beginning.

The contrast between Prospero and Mama Day is especially sharp with respect to gender politics. Though the relationship between Mama Day and her father Jean-Paul is portrayed as positive resource, it is nonetheless subordinate to the primary emphasis on strong female bonds—bonds that Miranda's isolation makes impossible in *The Tempest*. Mama Day's central drama concerns the recovery of connections with three women: Sapphira, the slave woman who originated the Day line; Ophelia, Mama Day's mother who, distraught over the death of her daughter Peace, drowned herself; and Cocoa, her grand-niece, who has left Willow Springs and works in New York City.

Like Mama Day, Cocoa has a double name that works to deny Shakespearean expectations. Cocoa is named Ophelia after her great grandmother, whose death by water recalls the destiny of Shakespeare's Ophelia in the male-dominated world of *Hamlet*. Cocoa's alternate name aids the process of exorcising the burden both of her great grandmother's demise and of the potential Shakespearean connotations. Mama Day's comment about tradition can be applied to the novel's general stance toward patriarchal political structures in *The Tempest*: "Tradition is fine, but you gotta know when to stop being a fool."

Shakespeare's *The Tempest* is a story with roots and Naylor's *Mama Day* recounts the lives of Miranda (Mama Day), her sister Abigail, Abigail's grown grand daughter, Ophelia (Cocoa), and her love affair and marriage. Cocoa's voice in the novel explores the tragic past of Mama Day's forebears as well as the preset in which Mama Day functions as healer and wise woman of the small community. Mama Day helps Bernice heal from misuse of fertility drugs and helps her conceive a baby through a combination of natural medicine and "helping nature out." Cocoa and George arrive in New York, marry, and eventually visit Willow Springs during which time the obsessively jealous Ruby imprisons Cocoa and works a spell on her that causes her to come quite near death. A powerful storm stops George and Cocoa in Willow Springs when the bridge collapses. George cannot believe the cause of Cocoa's illness and the means of her cure and dies in the process of trying to help her. Her sacrifice and Mama Day's healing powers combine to effect Cocoa's healings. The novel is constructed as conversation between George's spirit and Cocoa, looking back years after the event actually took place.

Willow Springs is a village on an island which is not to be found on any map; it is, in some sense, legally nowhere, because it is not claimed by a state. But it is somewhere: off the coast of Georgia and South Carolina, its pastoral opposes the city of the cities, New York. Unlike many other treatments of *The Tempest*, it takes Gonzalo's Commonwealth seriously, although it is matrilineal, matriarchal, and matrilocal. It also takes an advantage of certain aspects of inherited African beliefs, such as whether new-born babies are staying or going, and the importance of giving them a series of names, which helps situate part of the culture of the book. This aspect of the book marks a change which opens out new areas. George has risen highly in the world, but at great cost. Clearly, the highly competitive, egocentric, racist, and male-dominated world of New York Manhattan requires certain ruthlessness and focused determination for an African American male to succeed. And George has become a wealthy entrepreneur. But his one-sided emphasis on achievement has gained him status and riches, yet led him away from wholeness of self, as his lack of empathy for and understanding of women demonstrates. In gaining the world, George has risked his soul.

Cocoa, the unwitting victim of Ruby's jealousy over Junior Lee, has been hexed with a herbal poison. In her illness, Cocoa must depend on George to save her, but because of a hurricane, George cannot bring her doctors and traditional medicine; instead, he is asked to save Cocoa in Miranda's "way," but she gives him bizarre and inexplicable instructions. Like a lost child in a fairly tale, George must rely on an elderly woman whose advice seems to him irrational and irrelevant. But Miranda's words are patently symbolic and are essential for him to achieve his maturity. At this point in the novel, Naylor abandons realist conventions and adopts a mythic or parabolic mode, similar to the non-realistic style of *The Tempest*. It is a mistake to read this section of the novel—George's quest to the hen-house—literally. Naylor instead shifts the novel's progress to another level, moving from a provisional realism to a mythic plane—what is often described in contemporary criticism as "magic realism."

Shakespeare's plots emphasize the importance of transformative experiences. Naylor's narrative impels George to revise entirely his world picture. Because of his tortured childhood, George is only half a person. A good man who has the potential to become whole, he must undergo a fundamental change in character. George must value his own feelings, and those of others, much more than he does. Both Shakespeare and Naylor shape their action to underscore the necessity of appreciating a wider range of experience, one that embraces the joy of life, but also the irrational and the terrible. In *The Tempest,* Prospero must undergo change to be whole—as must Miranda, Ferdinand, and Antonio. But Caliban refuses to acknowledge even rudimentary structures of rationality; in *The Tempest,* Caliban resists change and refuses to undergo transformation. He cannot accept a different interpretation of the world, one that acknowledges order, reason, and a cosmic structure that is identifiably European.

George is Naylor's revised Caliban, but George's condition is the inverse of Caliban's. While Caliban resists reason and a patriarchal order, George resists emotionality and Miranda's vision of life. Caliban and George share several narratological features: Both lose their mothers; both are dispossessed because of their losses; both enjoy ardent sexual desire; both become drunk, and then give their allegiance to false leaders (Caliban to Stephano and Trinculo, George to Dr. Buzzard). But their most significant similarity is that George, like Caliban, refuses the possibility of his transformation.

Naylor's *Mama Day* is in relation with two different contexts, both of which are important for a full view. Naylor's departures from Shakespeare—especially her rejection of the absences and restrictions imposed by Shakespearean images of women—are substantial. By countering Shakespeare, Naylor demonstrates the degree to which Shakespeare does not author us, the extent to which that role has irreversibly passed to other. New problems indeed arise, but they are not Shakespeare's problems nor does his work contain the materials needed for exploring all the possible options. Both Shakespeare and Naylor are different in race, gender, time, and space. The fundamental struggle of life is to connect with the mysterious voices within ourselves—voices too often muffled by the roar of social conventions, regionalism, racism, and sexism.

Works Cited

Naylor, Gloria. *Mama Day*. New York: Ticknor & Fields, 1988.

Gates, Henry Louis Jr. *Race, Writing and Difference*. Chicago: University of Chicago Press, 1985.

Storhoff, Gary. "The only Voice Is Your Own: Gloria Naylor's Revision of

The Tempest." *African American Review* 29.1 (Spring 1995): 35-45.

Mukherjee, Bharathi. "There Are Four Sides to Everything." *The New York Times Book Review* (21 Feb. 1988): 7.

Dehn, Missy K. "Toward a New Order: Shakespeare, Toni Morrison, and Gloria Naylor's *Mama Day*." *MELUS* 19.3 (Fall 1994): 75-90.

11

Masculine Traits in the Feminine Self: An Archetypal Approach

— Geetha Sentthilkumar, P. Ambika and K. A. Krishnalalitha

Carl G. Jung used archetypes to illuminate personality and literature and suggested the existence of universal content forms that channel experiences and emotions resulting in recognizable and typical patterns of behaviour with certain probable outcomes. Thus in fictional narratives, it is assumed that characters with strong archetypal features will automatically or unconsciously resonate with a large audience. According to Jung's psychological framework, archetypes are innate universal prototypes for ideas and may be used to interpret observations. They are elemental forces, which play a vital role in the creation of the world and of human mind itself. Jung found these archetypal patterns and images in every culture and in every period of human history.

Jung has outlined archetypes into five main types: Shadow, Anima/Animus, Self, Ego and Persona. Shadow is the personification of that human, psychic possibility that we deny in ourselves and project onto others. Anima is an autonomous psychic content in the male personality, which can be described as an inner woman whereas Animus is an unconscious masculine component in women. Jung's third type of archetype, Self, refers to the regulating centre of the psyche which facilitates individuation. Ego, on the other hand, is the centre of consciousness. By Persona, Jung means, the mask that one puts on before one shows oneself to the outside world.

Jung believes that every person has qualities of the opposite sex not only in the biological sense but also in the psychological sense of attitudes and feelings. He attributes human rational thought to be the male nature, while the irrational aspect is considered to be female nature. Jung emphasizes this aspect in his work *The Syzygy: Anima and Animus:*

> Woman is compensated by a masculine element and therefore her unconscious has, so to speak, a masculine imprint. This results in a considerable psychological difference between men and women, and accordingly I have called the projection-making factors in women the animus, which means mind or spirit. (*Collected Works* 9: II par. 27 f)

Shakespeare reflects the English Renaissance stereotypical men and women and their various roles and responsibilities in society. He also questions, challenges, and modifies those representations. His stories provide opportunities not only to understand Renaissance culture better but also to accost our own contemporary generalizations about gender, especially what it means to be female. In his plays, he seems to have been raising questions about the standard images of males and females, the characteristics of each gender, and how each gender possesses both masculine and feminine qualities.

For Shakespeare, as well as for most of Renaissance society, women represented obedience, silence, chastity, piety, humility. However, gender characteristics were socially constructed and there was an easy cross-over of masculine and feminine traits to both genders. The Renaissance not only defined female roles, but it also clearly assigned certain behaviour to males. It is easy to see that the male had a place and a role to play, just as the female had a lesser place and a role. The woman is either in the house of her father like Juliet in *Romeo and Juliet* or in the house of her husband as Lady Macbeth in *Macbeth.*

Shakespeare rises above the conventional views of Renaissance society as he portrays women as more than passive characters. As an exceptional woman in Shakespeare's time, Queen Elizabeth I ruled Britain from 1558 to 1603. During her reign England underwent great changes and witnessed prosperity. Her contribution to the country proved that women could also be outstanding, knowledgeable and masculine. Her qualities, as Angela Pitt points out, are "fearlessness, courage, toughness, arrogant defiance and a provocative defense of territory" (29). Shakespeare was influenced by these qualities of the queen while creating his brilliant heroines.

The heroines of romantic comedies like Beatrice in *Much Ado about Nothing,* Rosalind in *As You Like It,* and Viola in *Twelfth Night* reflect this blend of feminine and masculine attitudes and behaviours. As strong females, they demonstrate more self-awareness than the men. They are able to control the action just as Portia, for example, who controls the final scene of *The Merchant of Venice* by bringing about the downfall of Shylock. Viola chooses a man of her choice by acting literally as both male and female, and cleverly controlling the Duke's relationship with Olivia. Like Portia, Rosalind dominates the action in *As You Like It.* She is intelligent, strong of character, patient, and is talented enough to organize four marriages. Portia and Rosalind have donned a masculine disguise which not only grants these heroines the freedom of movement and authority, but also makes their gender identity ambiguous.

Lady Macbeth, in the play *Macbeth,* is at some point masculine in her actions. She tackles even the highly critical situations using her wit. She wants her husband to become the king of Scotland. She feels that the fastest way for Macbeth to become the king is by murdering Duncan. She forces Macbeth to kill Duncan. Lady Macbeth would have killed Duncan by herself, but the king resembled her father as he slept, so she forces Macbeth to carry out their plan of murder. Her purposefulness is pure and her boldness is expressed in these lines:

> Infirm of purpose!
> Give me the daggers. The sleeping and the dead
> Are but as pictures; 'tis the eye of childhood
> That fears a painted devil. If he do bleed,
> I'll gild the faces of the grooms withal
> For it must seem their guilt. (2. 2. 52-57)

Robert Kimbrough argues in his article "Macbeth: The Prisoner of Gender" that Lady Macbeth wants to become cruel, which she considers to be a masculine trait. However, in order for her to become cruel she must cut off the flow of blood to her heart, which is the seat of love, the source of remorse, pity and compassion which are all attributes of human nature. Macbeth and Lady

Macbeth often cannot go to sleep because of the crime they committed. But still, Lady Macbeth is able to maintain her sanity and composure during the day, even more than her husband. She urges him to be light-hearted and merry. Once she practically rescues Macbeth from the frailty of his own conscience. When Macbeth sees Banquo's ghost, Lady Macbeth creates an excuse to explain his odd behaviour. When the situation grows worse, she takes charge once more and promptly dismisses the lords from the feast.

Portia, in *The Merchant of Venice,* is also an example of animus. She is able to experience the freedom of a male-oriented society where women do not ordinarily have a voice. The court, in which a disguised Portia defends Antonio, is completely devoid of women, except for the two female characters (Portia and Nerissa) who are clothed in a very sophisticated male disguise. The male disguise allows Portia to identify with the animus: the female equivalent of the anima. In disguise, Shakespeare's heroines reveal their masculine characteristics. For instance, Portia's masculinity is constructed through her lawyer-garments and masculine behaviour. Before leaving for Venice to enter the court room, Portia talks with her maid Nerissa about her disguise:

> . . . in such a habit,
> That they shall think we are accomplished
> With that we lack. I'll hold thee any wager,
> When we are both accoutred like young men,
> I'll prove the prettier fellow of the two,
> And wear my dagger with the braver grace. (3. 4. 60-65)

Rosalind is the strongest of all of Shakespeare's female characters. She convinces Celia that male disguise is best suited for her than anyone else. She says:

> Were it not better,
> Because that I am more than common tall,
> That I did suit me all points like a man? (1. 3. 116-18)

She convinces Orlando to come and woo her everyday and while he does this she advises him on how to be a better mate. The fact that they were in the forest and that she was disguised as a man allows her to claim her ability to exorcise his emotions of love that are torturing him and effectively tame him. Rosalind trains Orlando to be a better husband while she is disguised as a man in the forest. Orlando believes that this gentleman is simply helping him cure his own lovesickness.

There are several female characters throughout Shakespeare's plays that represent strong, intelligent and free-willed beings. Through their discourse, these women often show a mental capacity that is not only equal to that of a man's, but at times it can also be shown as superior. They also use their linguistic wit to argue with men in order to attract one who is an equal in the realm of intelligence and self respect. As George Gordon points out in his book, *Shakespearean Comedy and Other Studies*:

> A certain clear headedness, a frankness in facing facts, and a power of deciding what is to be done, are the peculiar and distinguishing marks of Shakespeare's happy women. . . . All women probably agree with Shakespeare. He does them more honour. He pays them the high compliment of supposing that they may have knowledge, shrewdness, wit and courage without ceasing to be wholly feminine and object of desire. (52)

This ability to express oneself with such clarity proves the idea of these women's self-awareness. They know what the society expects, but they also know their own minds. Shakespeare's idea of women was very much in contrary to that of Elizabethan society in that they believed women were not only inferior to men, but also possessions of men. It is for this reason that Shakespeare used gender disguises and humour in order to allow his female characters their freedom of speech and their right to refuse the constraints imposed upon them by men in such a society. In the light of Jungian theory, we have tried to analyse the female characters (Portia, Rosalind and Lady Macbeth) in Shakespeare's plays bringing out the unique reality of their gender construction and their contributions in unfolding the complexities in their society.

Works Cited

Gordon, George. *Shakespearean Comedy and Other Studies*. London: Oxford University Press, 1944.

Jung.C.G. *The Syzygy: The Anima and Animus.* Collected Works. <http://www.jungcircle.com/muse/lexicon.html>

Kimbrough, Robert. "Androgyny Seen Through Shakespeare's Disguise." *Shakespeare Quarterly* 33.1(1982): 17-33.

Pitt, Angela. *Shakespeare's Women.* London: David and Charles, 1981.

Shakespeare, William: *As You Like It: Six Plays.* Ed. George Gordon. London: Zephyr Books, 1946.

———. *The Merchant of Venice: Four Comedies.* Ed. David Bevington. Toronto: Bentam Books, 1988.

———. *Macbeth* < http://shakespeare.mit.edu/macbeth/full.html>

12

Masculinity and Disguise: A Study of Portia and Viola

— N. Chandra

The term "masculinity" generally means "the quality of being masculine" and the term "masculine" can be defined as "having the qualities or appearance considered to be typical of men; connected with or like men" (Hornsby). Masculinity is an opposition to femininity and is usually studied by comparing both. The prime criteria governing this construction of masculinity and femininity are power relations, division of labour, and social organization of sexuality and attraction. In Connell's words:

> Masculinity is socially constructed and has a material existence at several levels: in culture and institutions, in personality, and in the social definition and use of the body. It is constructed within a gender order that defines masculinity in opposition to femininity, and in so doing, sustains a power relation between men and women as groups. (Connell 454)

It is general assumption that only men have these traits. Later, during studies on masculinity, critics have claimed that it is not an innate feature of men; at times men don't even possess it and yet at other times women too may display these traits. Beynon's statement further clarifies this when he states, "Men are not born with masculinity as part of their genetic make-up; rather it is something into which they are acculturated and which is composed of social codes of behaviour which they learn to reproduce in culturally appropriate ways" (Beynon 2). It has to be realised that when women possess these masculine traits, they do not exhibit them, as they are culture-bound. The aim of the paper is to analyse the masculine traits of women in the Elizabethan and Jacobean periods as portrayed in Shakespeare's plays and how disguise helped women to prevail over their femininity. Portia in *The Merchant of Venice* and Viola in *Twelfth Night* are chosen for the study. The paper attempts to establish that by being intelligent, sarcastic, romantic, and determinant and by seeking free will, these two women are able to exhibit their masculinity while in disguise.

In *The Merchant of Venice,* Portia is an heiress in Belmont and her father has kept a lottery of caskets to decide on a suitor for Portia's marriage. She wants to marry Bassanio, so she gives clue to him and finally he selects the right casket to marry her. Antonio, a merchant and friend of Bassanio is in trouble when his bond to Shylock, a Jew, gets matured. He could not return the money to Shylock, which he borrowed and according to the bond if he fails to return the money on time, Antonio has to give one pound of flesh from his chest. When Shylock is strict to his bond, Portia goes to the court in disguise, as a judge and saves Antonio by ordering Shylock to take exactly one pound of flesh without shedding blood, and she claims that it is what was mentioned in the bond.

Viola and Sebastian in *Twelfth Night* are twins and are born in a noble family of Messaline. They get separated in a shipwreck and think the other is dead. Viola disguises herself as Cesario, a page-boy, and works under the duke of Illyria since she has no other option to manage in a new place. The duke is in love with Olivia, a countess, who has decided to mourn for her brother's death seven more years. When Viola negotiates with Olivia on behalf of the Duke, she falls in love with Viola, who is disguised as Cesario. By chance, Olivia meets Sebastian, Viola's brother and gets married to him. The duke understands Viola's love and they also get married.

In *The Merchant of Venice,* Portia is quick-witted, has high sense of morality and intelligence and uses free-will, all of which constitute the characteristics of men. When she is unable to exhibit such masculine qualities perfectly as a woman, she feigns them better in disguise. The male attire gives her much more confidence to demonstrate her masculine nature. She tells her maid Nerissa:

> When we are both accoutred like young men,
> I'll prove the prettier fellow of the two,
> And wear my dagger with the braver grace . . .
> Into a manly stride, and speaks of frays
> Like a fine bragging youth, and tell quaint lies. (3.4.60-65)

She is much more intelligent than all the male characters in the play. In the lottery scene, Bassanio could not make out the right casket, whereas she gives indications to him so that he can easily decide on the right casket. Monica Hamill in *Poetry, Law and the Pursuit of Perfection: Portia's Role in 'The Merchant of Venice'* criticizes this as: "He wins the lottery not because he is a better moralist than the other suitors, but because he does not try to rationalize the choice of lead" (236). Even in the last scene, both Bassanio and Antonio never try for a device to escape from the cunning bond of Shylock; Antonio is getting ready for his death whereas Portia uses her intelligence and shrewdness to liberate him from the clutches of Shylock.

With her intelligence, Portia overcomes the problem of getting the suitor of her preference. She could not violate the words of her father that she should not favour anyone regarding her suitor's selection for her marriage. She confides this to her maid Nerissa: "I may neither choose whom I would nor refuse who I dislike; so is the will of a living daughter curbed by the will of a dead father. Is it not hard, Nerissa that I cannot choose one nor refuse none?" (1. 2. 25-29). Even then she gives clues to Bassanio because she is determined to get married to him. She has not violated her father's wish and she has done what she wanted to do. Phyllis Rackin, in his article "Androgyny, Mimesis, and the Marriage of the Boy Heroine on the English Renaissance Stage," claims that Portia ". . . wins her desired husband, her intelligence enabling her to circumvent the stipulations of her father's will without actually breaking her oath" (448). The court scene validates her craftiness and diplomacy; especially when she talks on "mercy" everyone is impressed except Shylock.

Though she exhibits her intelligence throughout the play, she, it seems, is able to exercise it to the highest level only when she is disguised as a man. When Antonio is in trouble, even Bassanio, does not know the way to save his friend, Portia studies the bond and devices a solution. Antonio's ships failed to return on right time and Shylock refuses to get the money back since the time is over and he wants to go with the content of the bond by demanding a pound of flesh. Though all the men in the court do not know how to save Antonio, Portia comes there disguised as a judge to rescue Antonio. Had not Portia disguised as a man nobody would have accepted her argument and judgement as something wise. Hence here disguise provides her the necessary atmosphere to be acceptable to society.

When Portia enters the court in disguise, all believe that the judge is a man. This might be because the society may not accept the idea of a woman in the court or there might not be any woman judge in that period. In the beginning of the trial scene, she seems to be on the side of Shylock saying that the court has to follow the bond strictly. Shylock becomes happy that the judge is supporting him and he starts praising her as second "Daniel," which means she is the best judge. Then she starts speaking on "mercy" and asks Shylock to give some relaxation in the bond. When Shylock refuses, she cunningly plays her cards. She says Shylock has to be ready with his knife to cut the flesh without blood and not more or less than one pound of flesh has to be cut. In the judgment she cleverly manipulates to get some of Shylock's property to his son. She also refuses to give back the money Antonio borrowed from Shylock, when Bassanio is ready to give it. In disguise, her thinking remains positive and her judgement is widely accepted and praised by the public. She proclaims her masculinity by not doing the least favour to Shylock and threatens him with death for violating the law. Such aggressiveness is a common trait found in masculinity which Portia seems to adopt with much ease.

Further, Portia's sarcastic comments and behaviour make her more masculine. This is explicit in her comments on her previous suitors. Her treatment of Shylock shows her acerbic nature. Though she is acerbic towards Shylock, she is affable to his children. She gets Shylock's property to his son and she readily accepts Shylock's daughter Jessica's marriage with a Christian.

Though some of the critics say that Portia is not so wise to prepare the arguments and judgment against Shylock, and it was written by Bellario, the real judge, even then she has the courage to overcome the problem favourably using the written statements of Bellario. In that case, she demonstrates confidence in the way she carries herself through the course of the trail. Her disguise gives her added authority to remain masculine for a while and she makes good use of the opportunity. Though, the ring scene at the end of the play shows her feminine nature, her way of threatening her husband playfully, in front of others once again establishes her masculinity. Yet she surrenders herself to her husband Bassanio perhaps because she can not or does not wish to totally shed her feminity:

> One half of me is yours, the other half yours –
> Mind own, I would say; but if mine, then yours,
> And so all yours. O, thee naughty times
> Put bars between the owners and their rights! (2.2.34-37)

Viola in *Twelfth Night* is also disguised as a man and she, by being determinant and romantic, upholds her masculinity. Rackin states, "Viola has all the romantic instincts; shows all the intelligence" (448). She is new to the place and she feels safe and comfortable as a boy in the new place to work for Orisino, the duke of Illyria. Viola is very feminine in nature and she herself thinks that she cannot fit the disguise of a man. Malvolio comments on Viola in the disguise of Cesario as "Not yet old enough for a man, nor young enough for a boy; as a squash is before 'tis a peascod, or a codling when 'tis almost an apple: 'tis with him in standing water, between boy and man" (1.5.165-68).

Once Viola becomes a page-boy to Orsino, the duke, she is sent as a messenger to Olivia, to express the duke's love to Olivia. Many of such messengers walked away, failing in the attempt, because Olivia strictly rejected them. But Viola could meet Olivia and woo her successfully for the duke's sake. In Casey Charles's words, Viola "... as a self-conscious male mediation between man and woman, s/he becomes a better—a more eloquent, persuasive—man than the man s/he represents" (131). She becomes more romantic and she thinks and behaves as if she is a man and recites rhapsodically, as a representative of the duke, romantic poems to Olivia. Olivia falls in love with her and describes Viola as a lion and the duke as a wolf. "If one should be a prey, how much the better/To fall before the lion than the wolf!" and she continues saying that "Your [Viola's] wife is like to reap a proper man." Viola makes Olivia to get rid of her veil and whenever she is meeting Olivia, she becomes a man and when Olivia expresses her love for her, Viola regrets for gender mischief and says: "Disguise, I see, thou art wickedness."

Viola, by being self-determined than any other man in the play, proves her masculine nature. Kimbrough points out: "Viola experiences human freedom and growth in male disguise" (28). Firstly she has the courage to work under the duke, though she is a woman and she is not troubled in case the truth is revealed. Secondly, when the duke explains that his love is the greatest one in the world than any other woman's, she objects pointing out that woman's love is in fact the greatest and she tells her own love to the duke in the third person. Finally, she is a stranger to get her love consummated. When other characters such as Orsino, Sebastian, Viola's brother and Olivia could succeed in their love, it is Viola who has bedrock determination about it and finally she achieves it. In that case, no other man is as determined as Viola and she emphasises this as: "Who'ver I woo, myself would be his wife."

Obviously, Both Portia and Viola use disguise but Portia seems to be stronger than Viola. This might be because Viola fails to represent her masculinity sometimes: an instance is at Olivia's home, when she is called for a sword fight with Andrew. Since she could not fight, Sebastian fights for her. She is scared to tell that she does not know it. She tells in an aside: "Pray God defend me! A little thing would make me tell them how much I lack of a man." In another incident, the clown of Olivia tells Viola that she has to get a beard, which means she is lacking manliness and even her appearance betrays her femininity. The clown remarks: "Now, Jove, in his next commodity of hair, send thee a beard!"

When we compare both Viola and Portia, in disguise they enjoy the power of man as a judge or as a messenger of the duke. Both go for a common man's disguise to avoid the suspicion of the public by their voice or through some of their feminine attitudes. Portia happily chooses it and is invulnerable; whereas Viola was left with no choice and is vulnerable. Portia after revealing her disguise remains the same and Viola feels little uncomfortable when her disguise is revealed, she is totally silenced and wants to use the woman's garment immediately to get back to her identity.

To conclude, both Viola and Portia, if they do not get into the problem of gender identity, they are comfortable and once their disguise is revealed they lose their equilibrium. Therefore, women in disguise feel more comfortable to depict reality and do what they want to. They are society-bound to do the same when they remain as women so they use disguise as a tool. Gulick strongly points this out: "... in "Shakespeare's plays women are portrayed not only as better than men but as more intelligent too" (447).

Works Cited

Ayano, Hamaldo. "Women and the Gender Boundary in the Elizabethan England." 26.02. 2009. <http://www.hulford.co.uk/dumycz.pdf>

Belsey, Catherine. "Shakespeare and the Sexual Masquerade." *Prallax* 5.1(1999): 59-61.

Beynon, John. *Masculinities and Culture*. Buckingham, U.K.: Open University Press, 2002.

Charles, Casey. "Gender Trouble in *Twelfth Night*." *Theatre Journal* 49.2 (May 1997): 121-141.

Connell, R.W. "A Whole New World: Remaking Masculinity in the Context of the Environmental Movement." *Gender and Society* 4.4 (Dec. 1990): 452-478.

Gulick. Sidney, L. "Was Shakespeare a Woman?" *College English* 15.8 (May 1954): 445-449.

Hamill, Monica J. "Poetry, Law and the Pursuit of Perfection: Portia's Role in *The Merchant of Venice*." *Studies in English Literature 1500-1900:* 18.2 (Spring 1978): 229-243.

Kimbrough, Robert. "Androgyny Seen Through Shakespeare's Disguise." *Shakespeare Quarterly* 33.1 (Spring 1982): 17-33.

Rackin, Phyllis. "Androgyny, Mimesis, and the Marriage of the Boy Heroine on the English Renaissance Stage." *PMLA* 102.1(Jan.1987): 29-41.

Shakespeare, William. *The Merchant of Venice*. Ed. E. C. Pettit. New Delhi: S. Chand & Company Ltd., 1997.

______________ . *Twelfth Night*. K.C.S. Madras: Desikan and Co., 1984.

13

Shakesqueer: A Queer Reading of Shakespeare

— M. Smitha

Queer theory and homosexual thought can be drawn back to Greek mythology where we discover that the great poet-musician Orpheus was a homosexual; the ancient seer Tiresius is a symbol of fluidity of gender. It is indeed shocking as well as fascinating to learn that the most popular and appealing author William Shakespeare was a bisexual. Hence, even though queer theorists and Shakespeareans were regarded as two separate groups of scholars, a queer reading of Shakespeare makes up for a unique and rare version of the Bard and his creation.

Queer theory, which emerged in the late twentieth century, was a bold and enduring challenge to the clichéd and superficial interpretations that had till then shaped the study of Shakespeare. This paper aims to decode (or demystify) the enigma called Shakespeare by applying the principles of queer theory to one of his most famous plays, *Hamlet*. The paper also includes a discussion of how a film-maker like John Madden, who adapts Shakespeare in his movies, discerns the homosexual ingredient through a couple of scenes.

When we trace the history of queer theory, we find that it grew out of feminist thought, post structuralism and post-modern theories. It focuses mainly on how sexuality was and is a product of culture, and not biologically inherent in human-beings. After having studied the work of Michel Foucault, the queer theorists concluded that sexuality is being socially constructed through various discourses of medicine, law and media studies. From the work of feminist philosopher Judith Butler, queer critics understand gender and sexuality as "performative acts," not essential identities. The work of Eve Kosofsky Sedgwick explores how hetero-homo binary opposition shapes so many different aspects of the Western culture. Thus a deconstructive notion is very much essential for queer theorists as the term "queer" gets destabilized and it encompasses all human sexual practices while rejecting the opposing binary hierarchies of gender, race sexuality and class that govern our culture and society. The politics of identity is completely disregarded by the queer theorists and the theory exploits the incoherencies of allegedly stable relations between sex, gender, and desire which identify heterosexuality. Queer theorists follow the work of Sigmund Freud and Alfred Kinsey and argue that the key binary oppositions are not fixed but are rather fluid and dynamic and socially defined positions.

An exploration of Shakespeare, the man and his works, provides ample reach for the queer theorists as well as psychoanalytical critics to label him as a gay. The Elizabethan England of the late sixteenth and seventeenth centuries considered same-sex love as socially prohibited behaviour and the offenders were even sentenced to death. So writers like Christopher Marlowe and Shakespeare were often compelled to write in codes in order to reveal homosexuality (Marlowe's *Edward II* is a good example). Queer theory re-evaluates the traditional way of viewing and criticizing art, a tradition that has consistently suppressed representations of sexuality and sexual orientations.

Viewing the Shakespearean play, *Hamlet* from a post-structuralist perspective, Hamlet's identity can be seen as a constellation of multiple and unstable positions, which is what the queer theory exactly does. It is a debunking of stable sexes, genders and sexualities. Was Hamlet gay? A very relevant question for pursuers of queer studies. The character of Hamlet, being the most compelling in all of literature, has given fodder for various interpretations. Hamlet had gained so much popularity that he had become the beloved of the audience and the readers. No one was ever ready to taint his character with a controversial remark. It was only during the twentieth century that Ernest Jones applied the psychoanalytic theory to *Hamlet* and alleged Hamlet of having been inflicted by Oedipal Complex. Later on, gay and queer critics discovered traits of homosexuality in Hamlet.

There are scenes in the play that one can choose to read from a queer perspective. The homosexual inclination of Hamlet unravels in his love for his confidante, Horatio. Shakespeare utilizes the key character Horatio to exhibit the underlying attraction which Hamlet feels for Horatio. Throughout the play, the most loving and endearing lines come form the mouth of Horatio when he speaks to Hamlet. He refers to Hamlet as "... sweet Lord. . . " and "my dear lord" (3.2. 53-56). Shakespeare pushes the point one step further by having Hamlet die in the arms of Horatio. There is a deep love revealed further, especially to a queer author, as Horatio calls out his "sweet prince" which could have a valid homosexual reading. We even come across Hamlet being accompanied by Horatio to important functions and this does not arouse any suspicion.

Hamlet fears of the stigma attached to male-male sexual desire and therefore restricts the expression of such sentiments creating an atmosphere where physical contact is impossible. With Horatio, Hamlet disrupts every moment of potential intimacy by interrupting himself and changing the topic of discussion to theatrical plays.

We also understand that Ophelia has the power to reveal the truth about Hamlet's sexuality. Many of Ophelia's lines can be interpreted as coded. In the "Mouse Trap Scene" Hamlet tells her "I did love you once" (3.1.92). Ophelia responds by saying that she believed he loved her and he cruelly says, "you shouldn't have believed me. . . I lov'd you not" (3.1.116-118). When Hamlet is impatient for the prologue to finish, Ophelia tells him "tis brief. . ." he curtly replies, "As a woman's love" (3.2.152-54). This coded line may mean that love between men is everlasting. It is another instance which contributes to Hamlet's queer behaviour. Ascribing to queer theory, Hamlet, the hero, loves another, and that is a male. Therefore it becomes evident why Hamlet does not marry Ophelia or to be more specific why Shakespeare doesn't allow Hamlet to get married to Ophelia. Hamlet's reason for denial is that he cannot marry her until he avenges his father's death. Ophelia is shocked by the kind of insane behaviour that he displays. The moral dilemma that Hamlet faces makes him a mysterious personality just like his creator.

Shakespeare's theatre employed only male actors to portray female characters leading to discussions of obscured sexual identity. The coding of Shakespeare and the anti-theatrical tracts in the play reveal cultural anxieties about candidly expressing any kind of illegitimate behavioural patterns that undermine social/ patriarchal institutions. In fact, the possibility that Hamlet is a homosexual has been denied and suppressed for years. The play, *Hamlet* is not only a product of implicit homo-eroticism but it also demonstrates how misogyny merges with homophobia, a cultural fear of male-male sexual bonding. The queer theorists argue that Hamlet seems to embody the specific juncture of misogyny and fear. He clearly shows misogynistic tendencies with Gertrude and Ophelia. Queen Gertrude has a coded line that can be read as a clue to Hamlet's homo-erotic true nature. The Queen expresses her hope that perhaps Hamlet is madly in love with Ophelia. She says, "And for your part, Ophelia, I do wish that your good beauties be the happy cause/ Of Hamlet's wildness. So shall I hope your virtues/Will bring him to his wanton ways again,/To both your honours" (3.1. 36-41). Gertrude exposes a mother's desire for her son to be hetero-sexual, marry a lovely woman, avoid possible imprisonment and scandal, produce heirs and make her a proud and happy grandmother. This thought stems out in her as she suspects Hamlet's sexual preference and continues to hope that it is not true. Hamlet also seeks meaning in the figure of the Norwegian prince, Fortinbras, a warrior-hero who becomes in Hamlet's eyes an icon of fully achieved masculinity.

In another instance,. there is Laertes who gives caution to Ophelia and this is again an intriguing matter for the queer critics. Laertes has something to say about Hamlet's sexuality to Ophelia. It reveals first-hand knowledge of Hamlet's sexual advances. There is an implication regarding homosexual relation between Laertes himself and Hamlet in Act 2 Scene 1 when Polonius goes to Reynaldo and asks him to spy on Laertes and spread rumours about him among his friends and acquaintances in France saying that Laertes drinks, gambles, fights and visits brothels (2.1.59). Polonius instructs Reynaldo to make it known that Laertes is a man's man. The intention behind such an action can be inferred to his anxiousness to protect Laertes's reputation as well as his own position in the kingdom.

The second scene in the play that illustrates the erotic-love triangle is when Hamlet and Laertes are engaged in a duel near Ophelia's grave. Each one claims that he loved her more than the other. Laertes leaps into the grave and Hamlet challenges his sincerity as he jumps into the grave and they begin to fight. Hamlet cries in despair, "I lov'd Ophelia. Forty thousand brothers/could not. . . make up my sum" (5.1.269-71). This scenario of two men set at odds by a woman clearly fascinated Shakespeare and it is an example of sexual tension between men being expressed in an apparently socially accepted way. The inherent homosexual attraction is clearly spelled out when we closely analyze the coding being used. Hamlet's effeminate tendency is evident when Claudius calls Hamlet's sorrow as "unmanly grief" (1.2.94); it shows that Hamlet's sexual preference is a crucial factor for his depression in the later stage of the play.

Many of the film makers and stage directors of modern times are deeply interested in this queer factor of Shakespeare. Some of the movies based on the adaptations of Shakespeare's works highlight the homosexual component contained in his works. Some films like, for example, John Madden's Oscar-winning *Shakespeare in Love* sheds light on the queer aspect of the Bard himself in a couple of instances. When Will hears Thomas of Kent (Viola) speak his own lines from *Two Gentlemen of Verona,* we perceive his intense attraction towards that voice speaking of true love with a novel passion even though Will was under the impression that it was a boy-actor enacting the scene. However, the film never allows any homoerotic story-line to unfold in it but it recognizes Shakespeare as a man with a homosexual element within him. Will soon recognizes Kent as a woman cross-dressed playing Romeo, and cross-dressed man playing Juliet, and then returning both roles to gender-appropriate actors (appropriate to modern audience, though inappropriate to Shakespeare's). The film renders the psychoanalytic development of Will from an immature homoerotic to a fully released heterosexual with remarkable precision albeit not explicitly.

The subject of homosexuality and gender in Shakespeare's plays and performances has long been a topic of critical interest.

Ranging from the humorous and the playful to the dark and the taboo, the explorations of human sexuality is a constant speculation in Shakespeare's texts. In the past, while it led some to censor it, the trend in modern scholarship has been to undertake a close analysis of his writing for the purposes of uncovering the cultural and historical factors behind his presentation of the sexes. As Richard Burt avers the queering of Shakespeare is not defined in terms of simply labelling the author as gay or bisexual, but of opening up a queer space of "overlapping kinds of knowledge and reading practices" (75).

Works Cited

Burt, Richard. *Unspeakable Shakespeares: Queer Theory and American Kiddie Culture.* New York: St. Martin's, 1998.

Caplan, David. *Questions of Possibility: Contemporary Poetry and Poetic Form.* London: Oxford University Press, 2006.

Shakespeare, William. *Hamlet.* Ed. Cyrus Hoy. Norton Critical Edition. Second Ed. New York: Norton, 1992.

14

Transvestism in Shakespeare

— S. Subhapriya

> In every human being a vacillation from one sex to the other takes place and often it is only the clothes that keep the male or female likeness while underneath the sex is very opposite of what is above (Woolf 172)

Transvestism is the practice of wearing the clothing of the opposite sex for emotional or sexual passion. Transvestism does not include all instances of wearing such clothing. Transvestites tend to perceive themselves either as women with masculine predispositions, or as men with comparable feminine predispositions. Transvestism is not limited to using the clothing of the other gender to elicit sexual excitement but also includes involvement in sexual behaviour to gain emotional satisfaction from dressing in the clothing of opposite sex. Transvestites often describe their behaviour as expressing those aspects of the identity and roles of the other gender that they feel are important aspects of their self definition.

This essay aims to compare transvestism in three different theatrical cultures: Elizabethan stage, Kabuki Theatre of Japan and Peking Opera of China with special reference to Shakespeare's *As You Like It*. The Elizabethan stage, Kabuki Theatre and Peking Opera practised transvestism through their boy actors, Onnagata and the Dans respectively. These actors were female inside the theatre and male outside of it. Each of these stage-cultures had explored transvestism in its theatre as a result of banning women from the stage. Each had different ways of presenting female that were culturally relevant and not. Why do we see in different cultures a trend towards transvertism in entertainment? Are they same or is there a difference? How was the role of female conveyed? How close was it to the cultural role of the female? This essay attempts to find answers for these questions.

Transvestism in Shakespearean theatre was multilayered and intricate. Shakespeare has a long history of transvestism in his plays which reflected the English theatre of the Elizabethan-Jacobean period. The phenomenon of boy actors playing women's part in Shakespearean comedy can be analyzed primarily along three affiliations. The boy actors are:

i) a portrayal of meta-dramatic theme of identity itself;
ii) merely a convention of a theatrical lineage of medieval drama;
iii) a political convention specifically necessitated by the determination to keep women off any public stage or platform.

Kabuki is one of the four forms of Japanese classical theatre which developed during more than 250 years of peace of the Edo Period (1600-1869). It is thought to have originated in the dance-and-light theatre first performed in Kyoto in 1693 by Okuni, a female attendant at the Izumo shrine. In the wake of its success, rival troupes quickly formed and Kabuki was born as drama and dance ensemble performed by women. Soon women began attracting the wrong type of men. In 1629 women were banned from appearing in Kabuki performance. So, young male actors known as Wakashu or Oyama took over. These young men could take the role of women due to less masculine appearance and higher pitched voices in comparison to adult men. Even then, audiences frequently became disorderly and brawls occasionally broke out leading the Shogunate to ban young male actors in 1652 who were replaced by matured men.

Beijing Opera or Peking Opera is a form of traditional Chinese theatre which combines music, vocal performance, mime, dance and acrobatics. It was originally staged for the court in 1790 and came into the public later. The Dan refers to any female role in Peking Opera. In the early years of Peking opera, all Dan roles were played by men. The ban on female performers also led to a controversial form of brothel, in which men paid to have sex with young boys dressed as females. Ironically the performing skills taught to the youths employed in these brothels lead many of them to become professional Dan later in life.

Even though these three stages use transvestism for entertainment, their method, intention and portrayal are different. Shakespearean plays present the complex desires and fantasies and mediated cultural anxieties. These desires and anxieties are not only gendered but erotic in their origination and implication. Costuming boys as women who might then impersonate men, was especially well suited for exploring the constructional and dissolution of identity. In the Kabuki portrayal, Onnagata naturalism gave way to exaggeration, a forced but refined femininity. The voice is pitched in a high falsetto, and hand and arm movements are constrained by the sleeves of the kimono which are small and tightly controlled. The Dans used to signify a unique "Chineseness" in contrast to the sense of culture presented in Japanese theatre. Within a short span of time, a varied range of emotions are displayed in an aesthetic manner. For example the concubine in the one act play, "The Favourite Concubine Becomes Intoxicated," begins in a state of joy, and then moves to anger and jealousy, drunken playfulness and finally to a feeling of defeat and resignation.

In the Kabuki, a woman is postulated as an idea rather than a nature. The actors perform the role of women with male actors bodies, constantly challenging the gender and power constructs of women as idealized mother/wives/mistress and men as work-focused bread winner. As a result the female role conveyed through the male-bodied cross-dresser did not appear to be transgressing social norms; rather he upholds and even shapes the traditional ides about the binary gender role system.

The Dan refers to any female role in Beijing opera. Their roles are divided into five subtypes: old women are played by "laodan," martial women are "wudan," young female warriors are "daomadan," virtuous and elite women are "qingui" and vivacious and unmarried women are "huadan." Mei Lan Fang, the pioneer in modern Peking opera, has introduced a sixth type of role the "huashan." This type combines the status of the qingui with the sensuality of the huadan. "Men are men, but Man is a woman," quotes Chesterton in his novel *The Napoleon of Notting*

Hill. He writes: "Individually, men may present a more or less rational experience, eating, sleeping and scheming. But humanity as a whole is changeful, mystical, fickle, and delightful. Men are men, but man is a woman."

In Shakespeare the female conveyed through the transvestite boy actor render unexceptionable and unthreatening female autonomy and erotic power for a predominantly male audience. If young boys are erotically compelling because of their femininity it is because they represent all of the attraction and none of the threats of female heterosexuality. Shakespearean transvestism is depicted through Rosalind/Ganymede, Viola/Cesario, Portia/Balthazar and Imogene/Page Boy. This paper takes up only Rosalind/Ganymede for analyzing Shakespearean transvestism and male homoeroticism.

The boy heroine is an androgyne, a fusion of sexes, "a figure of unfused, discretely layered gender identities, play-boy, female, character, male persona" (Shapiro 3), which is differently highlighted at different moments in *As You Like It*. It is first intimated by Rosalind's adoption of the name Ganymede when she decides to don male attire. Of all the male names available to her, she chooses the young lover of Zeus, familiar to the Greek and Latin literate Britons and as a colloquial term used to describe the male object of male love. James Saslow traces the artistic representation of Ganymede in western culture and remarks: "The very word Ganymede was used from medieval times well into the seventeenth century to mean an object of homosexual desire" (quoted in Traub141). It is also suggestive of plurality.

The figure of Rosalind dressed as a boy engages in playful courtship with Orlando acting out the parts scripted for women by her culture. Doing so does not release Rosalind from patriarchy but reveals the constructed nature of patriarchy's representations of the feminine and shows a woman manipulating those representations in her own interest, theatricalising for her own purpose that which is considered to be innate teaching her future life partner how to get beyond certain ideologies of gender to more enabling ones.

The role of Rosalind through her transvestism challenges and disrupts gender differences and securely repositions as object of exchange in a patriarchal social structure. Instead of being containing and even eliminating her female power Rosalind is empowered by her disguise. It is Celia who fabricates the primary escape plot. Only after her formulation of an elaborate plan does Rosalind add cross dressing to the list of transgressions:

> Were it not better,
> Because that I am more than common tall,
> That I did suite me all points like a man?
> A gallant curette axe upon my thigh,
> A boar spear, in my hand, and– in my heart
> Lie there what hidden woman's fear there will–
> (1. 3. 116-121)

This manner of transvestism helps Rosalind to break into a dual mode of desire. By means of her male improvising she leads the play into a mode of desire both heterosexual and homoerotic. Although she displays her desire for Orlando she enjoys her position of male object of Phebe's desire. The virtue of transvestism lays its stress on the word "if"—this can be analyzed through the scenes of courtship. Ganymede takes the lead in their courtship "if you say so, then I said so"; Orlando can woo and even wed Ganymede as "if thou wert indeed my Rosalind" and as 'if the marriage were real" (4. 1.189-90). "If" not only creates multiple possibilities and positions it also conditionally resolves the dramatic confusion created by cross-dressing that the play cannot sustain. Rosalind says to Silvius, Phebe and Orlando:

> [To Phebe] I would love you, if I could... I will marry you, if ever I marry a woman, and I'll be married tomorrow; [to Orlando] I'll satisfy you, if ever I satisfied man and you shall be married tomorrow;[To Silvius] I will content you, if what pleases you content you; and you shall be married tomorrow. [To Orlando] As you love Rosalind, meet: [To Silvius] as you love phebe, meet: and as I love no woman, I'll meet. (5. 2. 125-131)

Those desires which Rosalind is not able to express in the patriarchal structure are presented through the transvestite Ganymede. In the epilogue, Rosalind appeals directly to the taste of female audience members thereby demonstrating the contentment over what may have been a societal anxiety about women's visibility to other women. Evidently, Shakespeare basically used boy-disguised-as-girl-disguised-as-boy to make the transgressing female escape from the gaze of other females.

To sum up: Transvestite disguise which the Elizabethan stage, Kabuki Theatre and Peking Opera formulated does not blur the distinction between the sexes but heightens it in its own accord. This is due to the fact a heroine in male attire would stir up considerable anxiety, raise troublesome questions about sexual identity and gender roles but cross dressed heroine plays rarely provide any clear cut answers although the drive is towards aesthetic closure which demands un-disguising and celebrates heterosexual union.

Works Cited

Brandon, James R., William P. Malon and Donald H. Shively. *Studies in Kabuki: Its Acting, Music and Historical Context*. East West Centre: University of Hawaii Press, 1978.

Dolby, William. *A History of Chinese Drama*. New York: Harper and Row, 1976.

Kincais, Zoe. *Kabuki*. New York: Benjamin, 1975.

Mackerras, Collin. *Peking Opera*. New York: Oxford University Press, 1997.

Shakespeare, William. *As You Like It*. New Delhi: Macmillan, 1980.

Traub, Valerie. "The Homoerotics of Shakespearean Comedy." *Gender in Play on the Shakespearean Stage: Boy Heroines and Female Pages*. Ed. Michael Shapiro. New York: The University of Michigan Press, 1994

Woolf, Virginia. *Orlando*. Oxford: Oxford University Press, 1992.

15

Othello: A Study of 'the Self' and 'the Other'

— M. Parimala

Shakespeare's plays, though written four hundred years ago, have been subjected to various new theories of culture, politics, gender, race and other hierarchies. Such contemporary post-colonial theories are formulated on the basis of the colonizer-colonized relationship. It is, obviously, the discourse of the oppressed, the displaced, the marginalized, "the other." This paper attempts to discuss *Othello* in a postcolonial perspective with special reference to Edward Said's *Orientalism*. Post-colonial reading of the play *Othello* might offer insights into the power relations of the colonizer and the colonized and the Occident's construction of the Orient. Though "Shakespeare wrote at a time when English mercantile and colonial enterprises were just germinating" (Loomba and Orkin 1), yet, the play alludes to sixteenth century Europe and its colonial discourse. It symbolizes the English/ European domination and the victimization of colonized subjects. It also explores the inequities and racial discrimination that existed between "the self" and "the other".

In a post-colonial reading of the play, the reader could observe a vertical split in the character of Othello, the protagonist who is the embodiment of various binary oppositions. Othello, a man of colour, is greatly reputed as the general of the army in an alien country; enjoys all privileges that a white should enjoy; marries the "fair" Desdemona and claims Venetian citizenship; described as loyal, brave and honest—everything sounds strange for a Blackman! Moreover, he is praised as "fair" by the duke in the line "Your Son-in-law is far more fair than black" (1. 2. 29).

In a way, Othello is identified on par with the white citizens of Venice. He clearly attaches great importance to the image of himself as a unique/exotic figure. Loomba states: "Othello the Moor clearly has an African past and yet is also identified with the very Turks he goes to fight" (Loomba 13). Therefore, Othello is quite comfortably oblivious of his racial difference, until Iago vehemently emphasizes his "otherness." In the words of Burton:

> Othello moves from being a colonized subject on the terms of a white Venetian society and trying to internalize its ideology, toward being marginalized, outcast and alienated from it in every way until he occupies his 'true' position as its other. (Burton 57)

Edward Said's *Orientalism* states how the Western texts have represented the East and how it constructs the orient and the occident through fictitious descriptions. He also mentions how meticulously the colonizers convince their colonized subjects that their culture represented universal civilization. An Oriental reading of *Othello* exposes those false representations and informs the reader the true intention and the cunning nature of the colonizer through Iago and other characters. Even before Othello is introduced to the audience/readers, they are conditioned to censure Othello via Iago's construction who calls Othello as "the moor," "devil," "an old black ram," "a thief," "a rapist," "the thick-lips" and so on; Brabantio too condemns him as a person performing "magic" and "witchcraft." Iago's antagonism to Othello is not motiveless malignity. Iago who is aware of Othello and his indigenous culture could not stomach Othello marrying Desdemona and considers it as a racial intolerance. Iago is also grudged against Othello, a man of colour dominating him who is in relegation to Othello. Iago plans to deflate Othello's good familial relationship and to defame Othello's power and position. Further, Iago has a far-fetched suspicion that Othello has an adulterous affair with his own wife Emilia. Being jealous of Othello, Iago attempts to trap him by insinuating his suspicion to other characters like Roderigo, Cassio, Desdemona and Emilia and eventually Othello is entangled into his own jealous fantasies.

Iago is adept in manipulating and exploiting Othello and other characters to carry out his master plan forward without his direct involvement. He gradually implants the thoughts of suspicion, adultery and hypocrisy in Othello's mind and becomes responsible in revealing Othello's "savage madness" (4.1.52). Wherein Othello can be easily persuaded by Iago, the audience/ readers are made to believe Shakespeare's construction of occident that whites are civilized, learned and wise and diplomatic unlike the blacks, who are primitive and wild.

Iago becomes the true confidante of Othello by his fake "honesty," "learned spirit" and "those soft parts of conversation" (3.3.262-268), and towards the end Othello is thoroughly betrayed by Iago. When Iago accuses Desdemona of infidelity, Othello does not believe but later when Iago produces a "handkerchief" as proof, he could not endure his heart's pain and bursts into fury. This suspicion and jealousy implanted by Iago on Othello serves as the catalyst to trigger the "otherness" in Othello. Hence, Othello starts realizing himself as strange, indifferent, "the Other" and also indulges in "racial vocabularies" (Loomba 3) such as "false," "fair devil," "whore" etc., to curse his disloyal wife; in a way constructing his own identity as "other."

Since then, Othello realizes the true value of the handkerchief (the first token of love) that symbolizes his cultural heritage and loyalty, fidelity and chastity (of his mother) and her own, which he thinks being spoiled by Desdemona, his "self." Here the cultural displacement highlights how "the self" destroys "the other" imposed cultural heritage. Even before Othello could take any decision regarding Desdemona's disloyalty, Iago states "but let her live" (3. 3. 481), which indirectly connotes that Othello should kill Desdemona. Iago though not in a powerful position to dominate Othello, still he could exploit him by congesting his love and passion towards Desdemona that causes her death. Iago, who is aware of the fact that he cannot dominate Othello on state affairs, cunningly jams him in his domestic life by pushing him to the periphery. It is the cunningness of Iago that elevates him to the powerful threshold to exploit his "Other(s)" despite his powerless position when compared to Othello who is trustworthy and loyal and as relegated as powerless in spite of his powerful position. Innocent Othello without knowing Iago's tricks trusts him and promotes him to the Lieutenant's post. He also addresses Iago as "honest creature" (3. 3. 246) Iago is immensely delighted because his plan is getting succeeded. He says, "Work on my medicine, work: thus credulous fools are caught" (4.1.45).

Iago deceives Roderigo too (white against white), cheats him and later kills him after swindling all his property. Iago sacrifices friends who stand on his way to attain power and wealth. The line, "For gold and jewels, that I bobbed from him" (5.1.16), makes his intention clear. Othello becomes easy prey of Iago for power and Roderigo for wealth. Therefore, power and wealth induce Iago to perform all vicious deeds that in a way represent the hypocritical nature of the colonizer.

We feel sympathy for Othello who has been politically and emotionally exploited by Iago, only because Othello is his "other." Iago plays his role in such a convincing way that no other character can identify his malicious behaviour towards his enemies. Everyone believes him and at last all are deceived by the devastating consequences. We can also see how selfish the Duke and Senators are in leading him to his ruin. The duke is more concerned and conscious about his regime and the safety of his state rather than Brabantio's daughter's life. The Duke advises Brabantio:

> Take up this mangled matter at the best;
> Men do their broken weapons rather use,
> Than their bare hands. (1.3.173-175)

He and other senators support and encourage Othello to begin his married life with Desdemona in spite of his acceptance that:

> I have ta'en away this old man's daughter,
> It's more true, I have married her. (1. 3. 78-79)

He then shrewdly addresses Othello:

> Valiant Othello, we must straight employ you,
> Against the general enemy Ottoman. (1.3.48-49)

They are so good to Othello just to save their country Venice and the Islands, Cyprus and Rhodes, from Turks' invasion. The Turks are identified as blacks and by opposing them they invite inimical relations with the General of the Army (black against black). Thus Iago, the Duke and the Senators handle with ease the same method adopted by the colonizers to subjugate and exploit the colonized. Burton remarks: "He [Othello] is tripped of 'power and command' (5.2.329) and condemned to prison like an enemy of the State" (Loomba 58).

By such a postcolonial exploration of Iago and Othello, one can come to the conclusion that both deny the so called stereotypical traits of the Orient and the Occident. Iago being the occident comprises all viciousness in him such as wicked, malignant, bestial, hypocrite, crooked, self-centred and cunning; and stands contradictory to Othello, the black who has all the noble qualities, which are deliberately and wittingly exploited by Iago. But as far as the Moor is concerned, he is the amalgamation of "the Self" and "the other," with the embodiment of binary oppositions. Iago plays a significant role in making Othello realize his racial identity. Thus, though Shakespeare is kind to the marginalized people and gives them equal space and language to speak; at times he disgraces the coloured race and makes them the "Other." Nevertheless, we have to appreciate him for describing the embarrassing situation of the black race and its survival amidst the white.

Works Cited

Bartels, Emily C. "Othello and Africa: Postcolonial Reconsidered." *The William and Mary Quarterly* 54.1 (January 1997): 45-64.

Campbell, Lily B. *Shakespeare's Tragic Heroes*. London: Methuen, 1961.

Koot, Jan. *Shakespeare Our Contemporary*. London: Methuen, 1967.

Loomba, Ania. *Colonialism/Postcolonialism*. New York: Routledge, 2005.

Loomba, Ania and Martin Orkin (eds.). *Post-Colonial Shakespeare*. New York: Routledge, 1998.

Marsh, Nicholas. *Shakespeare: The Tragedies*. London: MacMillan, 1998.

Neill, Michael. "'Mulattos,' 'Blacks,' and 'Indian Moors': Othello and Early Modern Constructions of Human Difference." *The William and Mary Quarterly* 55.3 (May-June 1997): 361-374.

Reinelt, Janelle G and Joseph R. Roach. *Critical Theory and Performance.* New York: University of Michigan Press, 2007.

Said, Edward. *Orientalism.* New York: Vintage Books, 1979.

Schwartz, Elias. "Stylistic 'Impurity' and the Meaning of Othello." *JSTOR* 10.2 (Spring 1970): 297-313.

Shakespeare, William. *Othello.* London: Methuen, 1958.

16

Katharina Wronged? A Gender Study of *The Taming of the Shrew*

— V. Sangeetha

Shakespeare's *The Taming of the Shrew* opens with an "Induction"—a story that introduces the main drama of Katharina and Petruchio. The drunken tinker Christopher Sly is tricked by a group of callous young noblemen into believing that he is an aristocrat with a young wife. For his entertainment the play *The Taming of the Shrew* is performed. This factor has a key role to play in analysing whether Shakespeare wilfully denied Katharina her rights.

Katharina is a young woman who always speaks her mind out. She is rude and aggressive. She wants to have a husband, like her sister Bianca, but in her own terms. Her fiery temperament and headstrong nature has to be done away with. Her cross ways and scolding tongue have to be subdued. Shakespeare has the responsibility of enacting Katharina's metamorphosis in a lively way.

All dramatists are concerned with interesting their audiences, and all drama directly or indirectly reflects the taste and ideas of its own time. Shakespeare too was no exception. He focused on the Elizabethan audience. This play gives bold and amusing dramatic shape to controversial themes of immediate and permanent concern—love, courtship, the relation between husband and wife, the nature and role of women, the tensions of the battle of the sexes. In order to appreciate the play the attitudes and ideas prevailing in the sixteenth century has to be understood in addition to the fact that Christopher Sly represents the groundlings and recipes for keeping rebellious wives in order were sure of evoking boisterous guffaws from the Elizabethan groundlings.

Important attitudinal changes towards women and marriage developed during the sixteenth century. The long established idea of woman as man's inferior and his enemy sustained by strong Biblical authority was strongly challenged by the Reformation and the humanist movement. A new faith in the importance of the family and its special confidence in the nature of women began to blossom in spite of the continued limitations of women and her traditional subordination. Suspicion and fear of women claiming authority and challenging the ways of men continued. Gradually, towards the later part of the century the difficulties forced on women by their sexual and social roles began to be understood. The potential qualities of their nature were fully realized.

Changing attitudes towards women were inevitably caught up with changing ideas about marriage. Marriage was no longer a mere necessary evil for begetting children. It was thought of as an attractive personal relationship offering contentment of a high order through love and companionship. Marriage was celebrated as the foundation of all social order. However there was a unanimous stress in stating that authority in marriage lay entirely with the husband. The wife's primary duty of obedience demanded a thorough redirection of her will in his interests. Equally a wife's positive loving co-operation was a prerequisite for successful romantic marriage. Still husbands were enjoined to exercise their authority firmly in such a way so as to engage the active loving fellowship of their wives. However, women were not totally free to exercise their free will.

In such a prevailing scenario, Shakespeare has presented Katharina as a shrew. *The Taming of the Shrew* is a comedy written for the sixteenth century audience. It is a play that was ahead of its time in its views towards gender roles within society. Shakespeare's heroines are invariably powerful, bold, intelligent, pleasant, tactful and courageous—Portia, Beatrice, Cleopatra, Lady Macbeth, Cordelia to mention a few. When a great writer like John Ruskin says that Shakespeare has only heroines and no heroes, the thought has to be pondered. A person like Shakespeare who has given due respects to his female characters cannot ill treat or misrepresent women. Like Rosalind, Celia and Imogene,

Katharina is simply a character. Shakespeare views the whole story as a comedy to cater to the taste of the Elizabethans. A character like Katharina is sure to captivate the hearts of the audience. Shakespeare never had designs to humiliate or subjugate Katharina. By temperament she is a shrew; yet she has her dreams of getting married and leading a normal life. She is typically a woman of her times. She has no feminine aspirations. She wants a husband but not the one approved by her father. Unfortunately she is courted against her will by Petruchio, who is in Padua in search of a wife with a rich dowry irrespective of her looks and behaviour. Kate's dislike for Petruchio is ignored and the wedding solemnised. Critics are of the opinion that the female need to choose a partner is being denied and is brought under male control. It is not so. Katharina is not a male hating feminist. She too wants to fall in love, marry and lead a romantic married life—with a slight difference—in her own terms. When Petruchio fixes the marriage, Kate willingly gets dressed although with a sullen demeanour. A woman with such temperament like Kate could have easily refused to get married. Katharina is misunderstood by the Paduans. Baptista's restless and formidable daughter, known for her aggressiveness and petulant self-will, undergoes a deep humiliation in her role as a shrew:

> *Germino*: To cart her rather: she's too rough for me.
> There, there, Hortensio, will you any wife
> *Katharina*: I pray you, sir, is it your will
> To make a stale of me amongst these mates ?
> *Hortensio*: Mates, maid! How mean you that? No mates for you,
> Unless you were of gentler, milder mould. (1.1.55-60)

Paduans could neither cope with her nor value her fine nature. Her jealousy towards the more likeable Bianca springs from a genuine fear that despite her father's effort to help her find a suitor she may be condemned to spinsterhood. The encounter between the two in Act 2 is exciting. Petruchio is meeting for the first time the woman he has publicly committed himself to tame. Kate, both afraid of neglect and yet demanding in her expectations of men, is summoned to receive the remarks of an unknown suitor. In the battle of wits and wills which ensues between the two, both test each other's mettle and suggest indirectly the ideal image or the marriage partner they would value. Kate's attack reveals her admiration for intelligence and wit, manliness and courtesy, Petruchio indicates through a mixture of blandishment and insult his regard for gracefulness of presence. It seems they are destined for each other. He begins her taming with good humour but also with an unremitting and sometimes disconcerting rigour.

The Lord in the Induction explains to his serving man how a woman ought to behave, be courteous, humble, loyal and obedient. Induction acts as a suitable preparation for Katharina's character and her disgust for such stereotyping as well as her rebellion against Elizabethan society's gender values. In the sixteenth century, it was permissible for men to beat their wives. Shakespeare does not condone violence towards women, an accepted practice of the time. The play's attitude may be characteristically Elizabethan but is humanely expressed by Shakespeare.

While Kate displays physical abuse—in the tying together of her sister's hands, the beating of Hortensio with his lute, and the striking of Petruchio—Petruchio tames Kate by employing psychological tactics. He purposely misunderstands, dismisses and humiliates her. The tactics by which the exuberant and wilful Petruchio transforms Kate's obstinacy into obedience as well as the drama's undercurrent of violence and cruelty are at times unsettling.

Despite such limitations *The Taming of the Shrew* fascinates with its intriguing subject: the clash of sexes written for sheer comic relief. Petruchio's non-physical abuse which includes verbal and emotional abuse are ought to be viewed in a lighter vein. As Kate largely responds to Petruchio's cues it may be interpreted, that by its final act Kate is truly in love with her husband. Through supporting Petruchio's controlling use of language over Katharina, Tita French Baumlin in her article "Petruchio the Sophist and Language as Creation in *The Taming of the Shrew*" draws some very different conclusions from many other recent critics. She discusses Kate's relation to Petruchio as "not a sad image of lifeless surrender to male dominance, but a spirit of flirtatious fun that will generate a rich creativity in this marriage grounded upon self-respect, mutual respect, and proper care" (251).

The play does not invite the readers to take seriously Petruchio's actions and Kate's submission: the play is a kind of fantasy of male wish-fulfilment, which exists only in fiction. It is a demonstration that the gender roles played by men and women do not form part of their essential natures. The comic swapping of identities is only role-play. Tranio pretends to be Lucentio, the pedant pretends to be Vincentio; and Lucentio is in disguise as Cambio. Many of the characters are drawn from the stock types of the Italian *commedia dell'arte* (Davies 50). Consequently Kate's submission is very much an imaginary resolution of the conflict with her husband. Her final doctrinal speeches are at odds with the experienced needs of men and women that it is possible to bring such domestic harmony only in a make-believe world. Kate's behaviour right up to the end of the play represents her refusal to be categorized and controlled by the power structures by which men subordinate women. She refuses either to be silent or to submit herself as a passive public object for the male gaze. Her puns expose marriage as an unequal sexual exchange in which women are exploited to produce offspring for men with no benefits for themselves (2.1.194-205). She may be the object of his sexual innuendo, but she retains her dignity and has the last word. According to Lisa Hopkins, in her book *The Shakespearean Marriage: Merry Wives and Heavy Husbands* Kate has subverted the definition of taming through her speech at the end of the play. "Even in her meekness, she is not meek. Katherine may have been tamed, but she has very potentially, not been silenced; indeed she has just been given the longest speech in the play " (42). Harold Bloom sees Kate's final speech as ironic, proposing that she is explaining that in reality women control men by appearing to obey him. Katharina stoops to conquer Petruchio. Seemingly satisfying Petruchio's male ego, Katharina has the last laugh.

To conclude *The Taming of the Shrew* remains firmly optimistic: Petruchio and Kate stand harmoniously united in testimony to the youthful playwright's conception of the beauty and comradeship in the hands of a skilled and magnanimous artist.

Works Cited

Baumlin, Tita French. "Petruchio the Sophist and Language as Creation in *The Taming of the Shrew.*" *Studies in English Literature,* 1500–1900. 29: 23-257.

Davies S. *William Shakespeare: The Taming of the Shrew*. Harmondsworth: Penguin Books, 1995.

Hopkins, Lisa. *The Shakespearean Marriage: Merry Wives and Heavy Husbands*. New York: St. Martin's Press, 1998.

Newman, Karen "Renaissance Family Politics and Shakespeare's *The Taming of the Shrew*." *Shakespeare's Comedies*. Ed. G.Waller. Harlow: Longman, 1986.

Shakespeare, William. *The Taming of the Shrew*. Ed. R.C.Hood. London: Macmillan, 1975.

17

Redefining *Macbeth*

— C. Santhosh Kumar

It is essential to look at Shakespeare's *Macbeth* in a different perspective, contrary to the strongly believed and much discussed concepts. Over the years, Macbeth is portrayed as a downright villain with vaulting ambition. But won't it be right to argue that his unchallenging chivalry inspires him to attain greater positions in life?

This paper is an attempt in this regard—highlighting Macbeth's virtues and gallantry. It is argued that in the characterisation of Macbeth, Shakespeare takes a "noble" man, full of "conscience" and "the milk of human kindness" and makes of him a sinner, yet maintain him as a tragic hero with full stature commanding our sympathy at the end. It is also argued that it is Duncan's weaknesses, or, rather, his absurdities, which motivate Macbeth to kill him.

To comprehend Shakespeare's moral intention in the play, two things demand our careful observation—his use of supernaturalism in the play and scantiness of Macbeth's characterization. For *Macbeth,* we have one of the worst texts. The folio of 1623 offers a text which is thought to have been cut down for stage presentation. It is generally believed that Middleton was engaged on the occasion of some revival of *Macbeth* to adapt the play to a somewhat different form of entertainment, one in which there would be songs and dances by witches. Possibly to make room for ballet features, the precious dramatic craftsmanship was cut away. "Therefore. . . certain matters of the plot are inconsistent, and the story of Macbeth's reign is told more barely and scantily than one would believe possible in the author who had just written *King Lear*" (Craig 1043).

Hence, scholars have reasoned that if interpolations have been added, very likely Shakespearean portions have been cut down to make room for them. But this reasoning is far from conclusive. There are scholars who harbour the idea that any other than the Hecate passages are spurious. If this view is correct, then we are practically forced to the conclusion that *Macbeth* as first produced was just about as short (*Macbeth* is the shortest of all Shakespeare's plays, except one *A Comedy of Errors)* as in the Folio version. Doubtless there has been no loss of Shakespearean material.

However, from the preceding discussion it need not be concluded that the play of *Macbeth* is exactly as Shakespeare's final draft except for Hecate's part. There may be a few corrections in the Folio text. But present day scholarly opinion is that corruptions are probably very few, and that valid aesthetic principles will account for some features of the style of the tragedy which, in the past, were wrongly attributed to mishandling by scribes, the stage manager, an adapter, or the printers of the Folio.

Now that it is established that Shakespeare himself composed the supernatural parts in the play, it can be argued that he did it to satisfy King James. Lillian Winstanley states that *Macbeth* was "particularly designed to please King James" (quoted in Harbage 24). It is also on record that King James himself was a firm believer in witchcraft and was an authority on the subject to the extent that "when Reginald Scot wrote *The Discovery of Witchcraft* (1584) against the belief in witches, King James considered Scot's opinions 'damnable', and wrote his *Demonology* (1597) to confute them" (Craig 1045).

It has long been thought with very good reason that some of the witch-lore in *Macbeth* comes from accounts of various Scottish witch trials published about 1590. Scotch witches had the power of prophecy through their master spirits and were guilty of the practices described in *Macbeth.* They raised storms, beset vessels at sea, danced ceremonial dances in threes, made witch-broth quite like that in *Macbeth.* They were serious and dangerous creatures, and often deluded the unsuspecting by telling them partial truths. The "weird sisters," are thought of by Holinshed, from whom Shakespeare borrowed his materials for *Macbeth,* as "goddesses of destiny. . . nymphs or fairies," who had the knowledge of prophecy. In Shakespeare they are, however, of evil nature unlike the nymphs and fairies. It is still a question to what extent Shakespeare meant that the free will of Macbeth was interfered with by "supernatural soliciting."

In Holinshed's *Chronicle,* the Weird Sisters are "goddesses of destiny" derived from the heathen fatalism. In the play they are Elizabethan witches, their prescriptive powers subtly curtailed; they predict, abet, and symbolize damnation but do not determine it. Any sense that Macbeth is a helpless victim, his crime predestined, his will bound, is cancelled as the play proceeds. Nothing in the witches' prophecies would have suggested to an untainted mind that to "be king hereafter" (1.3.50) meant to be murderer first. That Macbeth was already tainted would have been apparent to the original audience. "The stars could influence but could not govern; the devils could come but only upon summons. At some unknown time for some unknown reason Macbeth has corrupted in pride, and has contemplated the sale of his soul as certainly as Faustus" (Harbage 20). When we later discover through the words of Lady Macbeth (1.5.18-20) that plans to murder Duncan had preceded the meeting on the heath, we should not bring charges of inconsistency or speculate about "lost scenes." Neither the Witches nor Lady Macbeth needs to be blamed for Macbeth's ambition to become the king. It is already in him. Harbage rightly points out, "The [Witches'] prophecies, nevertheless, without explaining or excusing Macbeth's crimes, impress us as mitigation: powerful and wily forces are speeding him on his course" (22). The Witches are, then, not the originators but the organizers of Macbeth's ambition.

As already indicated, Shakespeare went to Holinshed's *Chronicles* for the story of *Macbeth;* in the first instance to the account of the reigns of Duncan and Macbeth, in the second, to the chronicle of King Duff. From the former comes the story of Macbeth's rise and fall. From the latter he borrowed the story of how Donwald and his wife, the two whom King Duff never suspected, murdered King Duff in the castle of Forres. It is observed that Shakespeare treats the chronicles with great freedom, combining as he does the reigns of two different kings. Besides this great transposition, his most important changes are the increase in importance of the part played by Lady Macbeth and the development of the supernatural elements. The enlargement of the supernatural elements even beyond the superstitious *Chronicles* was already discussed. The remaining part of this paper concentrates on the trio Macbeth, Lady Macbeth and Duncan and attempts to justify Macbeth's motivation to annihilate Duncan.

Duncan is generally known to us as a "good king", but most particular characteristics are carefully kept from us. Booth remarks, "There is little for us to love or attach our imaginations to. We hear of his goodness; we never see it" (184). We find King Duncan a weakling, meek and humble—qualities inappropriate for a king. In *Macbeth* King Duncan is a venerable man, but too old to fight in battle beside his loyal thanes. He reminds Lady Macbeth of her own father: "Had he not resembled/My father as he slept, I had done't" (2.2.13-14). Shakespeare's "gracious Duncan" manifests deep emotions of love and gratitude which do not befit a king. He regards the rewards presented to Macbeth inadequate:

> O worthiest Cousin!
> The sin of my ingratitude even now
> Was heavy on me; thou art so far before
> That swiftest wing of recompense is slow
> To overtake thee. Would thou hast less deserved,
> That the proportion both of thanks and payment
> Might have been mine! Only I have left to say,
> More is thy due than all can pay. (1.4.14-21)

Duncan intends to reward Macbeth with greater things, maybe costly jewels, and his throne too—an underlying denotative and implied meaning cannot be ruled out. For Duncan, Macbeth is his saviour, one who protects the crown by defeating the invading enemy. For such a strong man Duncan's kingdom is due.

Duncan's visit to Macbeth's castle and spending a night away from the palace weakens his position. He surrenders himself to a kinsman who is his superior in many aspects. The king ought to have stayed back in his palace occupying his throne instead of placing himself at the mercy of Macbeth. At Macbeth's castle, Duncan's garrulousness is not suitable for an ideal king. Duncan tells Lady Macbeth; "Conduct me to mine host: we love him highly,/And shall continue our graces towards him" (1.6.1-3). He is over-sentimental and maudlin by over-emphasizing the strength and loyalty of his liegemen. His choice of a time to make his son Malcolm the king suggests his unintelligence. Altogether, Duncan is antithetical to Shakespeare's ideal of a good king in *Henry IV part I* where Henry of Bolingbroke counsels his son on the requirements of a noble king:

> By being seldom seen, I could not stir
> But, like a comet, I was wond'red at. . .
>
> My presence, like a robe pontifical,
> Ne'er seen but wond'red at; and so my state,
> Seldom but sumptuous, showed like a feast
> And won by rareness such solemnity. . . (3.2.46-47, 56-59)

The inefficiency of the king is supported by the prophecy of the three witches that Macbeth will be the king. In addition, the manoeuvring of Lady Macbeth helps Macbeth in achieving his ambition. Macbeth might not have nourished the thought of kingship had Duncan been par excellence and proved himself worthy of the throne. The unconscious mind of Duncan is exposed when he welcomes Macbeth with these words: "Welcome hither:/ I have begun to plant thee, and will labour/To make thee full of growing" (1.4.27-29). This speech is significant. "Duncan assures Macbeth that even if he had no inherent virtues to help him grow the former would force his growth, an unnatural rising to glory! Duncan has taken well in hand this process of the unnatural growth of Macbeth" (Dais 52). Edith Sitwell has suggested that Duncan himself was the motivator of ambition in Macbeth, which eventually led to the royal murder. Sitwell states, "Perhaps the good Duncan had planted ambition which was to be the cause of his own death in *Macbeth.*" (27).

Ambition in Elizabethan English denotes aspiration for power, but connotes always that the aspiration is evil. For an Elizabethan or Scottish general to aspire to be king would imply a willingness or desire to break the divine order in society and to take the power from one for whom Providence had designed it. Macbeth, therefore, has been guilty of the sin of ambition even before the Witches first speak to him. In the Elizabethan sense, murder and usurpation are public crimes, whereas ambition remains an unpardonable private sin. However, in today's world to aspire to be the ruler is laudable, for the power that is sought is delegated by the people only to one who they think has proved himself worthy of it.

It is important to study Macbeth's attitude to his wife because he is as much bound to his wife as he is loyal to his master, the king. He finds his wife reverberating his own kindled spirit: "Glamis thou art, and Cawdor; and shalt be/What thou art promised" (1.5. 16-17). Choosing between his master and his wife, Macbeth abets the latter as she is equal to him in every respect. "Lady Macbeth is ambitious, and loves her husband only as a worthy partner of her stirrings" (Ulrici 44). Lady Macbeth knows that her husband is honourable enough to acquire power. Her heraldry to her husband at his arrival back home heightens this impression:

> Great Glamis! Worthy Cawdor!
> Greater than both, by the all-hail hereafter!
> Thy letters have transported me beyond
> This ignorant present, and I feel now
> The future in the instant. (1.5.55-59)

She knows it is not chance but Macbeth himself who has brought him these honours by dint of his own manoeuvring (Ralli 331). According to Lady Macbeth, both these titles were conferred on Macbeth. Macbeth and Lady Macbeth find there is future in them whereas Duncan looks at future in Macbeth. Putting it another way, Macbeth finds a better partner in Lady Macbeth and Duncan is unequal to him.

Macbeth represents a typical Renaissance concept of the ideal man—to achieve more, and to aspire for greater position. Macbeth is praised by the king for his valour. The king calls him "valiant cousin" and "Bellona's bridegroom." This speaks in favour of Macbeth as a competent personality. Such an undisputed general has every right to occupy the throne whereas Duncan nominates his son as the successor. The king is blinded by the love of his children. He fails to see the legitimacy of Macbeth in ruling the land.

It is important to note that Macbeth never regrets that he has taken up the kingship except for a brief period immediately after the murder and just before occupying the throne. Even while uttering a philosophical outlook of life,

> Tomorrow and tomorrow and tomorrow
> We creep in this petty pace from day to day. . .
> A tale told by an idiot, full of
> Sound and fury signifying nothing.

we do not see Macbeth is grieving at all. Unlike Faustus, who is pained by his decision, Macbeth stands firm and resolute.

Works Cited

Booth, Wayne. "Shakespeare's Tragic Villain." *Shakespeare's Tragedies: A Selection of Modern Criticism.* Ed. L. Learner. Baltimore, 1963: 180-190.

Craig, Hardin, ed. *The Complete Works of Shakespeare*. New York: Scott, Forssmann & Co., 1951.

Hall, Calvin. J, Gardener Lindzey and John B. Campell. *Theories of Personality.* New York: John Wiley & Sons, 1957.

Harbage, Alfred. "Introduction." *Macbeth,* The Pelican Shakespeare. London: Pelican, 1956: 16-22.

Ralli, Augustus. *A History of Shakespearean Criticism,* Vol. I. London: OUP, 1932.

Sitwell, Edith. *A Notebook on William Shakespeare*. London: Macmillan, 1948.

Ulrici, Herman. *Shakespeare's Dramatic Art*. Tr. Alexander James William Morrison. London: Chapman, 1846.

18

Hamlet's Insanity as Defence Mechanism

— K. Ravichandran

Because of his deep understanding of human nature, his compassion for all types of people and the power and beauty of his language, William Shakespeare is regarded as the greatest writer in English. Shakespeare's plays continue to be read widely and performed throughout the world. They have the same powerful impact on today's audience as they had when they were first staged. No other writer in English has won such universal and enthusiastic praise from critics and contemporaries.

Shakespeare's instinct and interest to study human psychology made him record in his plays not only normal human behaviour but also the abnormal. Hallucination, sleep-walking, violent fits of anger, jealousy and imbecility are some types of abnormalities which Shakespeare has dealt with in his plays. But it is madness, real or feigned, which attracted him the most. He has dealt with various kinds of insanities in a number of his plays like the madness of Portia in *Julius Caesar* and Malvalio in *Twelfth Night.* However the most skilful handling of madness is to be found in *King Lear* and *Hamlet.* This article is an attempt to analyse Hamlet's madness.

The problem of problems in Hamlet is the predicament of Hamlet's insanity. Critics have expressed four different views on his insanity. The first view is that Hamlet is sane throughout, but feigns insanity. The second view is that he is sane earlier but becomes insane only after his interview with the ghost. The third view is that he is neither insane, nor does he feign insanity. The fourth view is that his madness is less than madness and more than feigned.

Hamlet's violence at Ophelia's grave where he exhibits oodles of opposite emotions is a remarkable instance of his want of self-control. The queen describes him:

> This is mere madness;
> And thus awhile this fit will work on him;
> Anon, as patient as the female dove,
> When that her golden couplets are disclosed,
> His silence will sit drooping. (5.1.307-311)

Though Hamlet's insanity on this occasion is prompted by his anxiety to excuse his violence, his raving over the grave is not mere pretension. It is real. In fact, this passage is the best card that the believers in Hamlet's madness need to play—He is reedy, almost mad with grief as well as anger. He is full of "wild rage" and "sick despairs" at this wretched world which drives him to such deeds of misery. If we realize the situation, it is clearly explicit that Hamlet has chosen madness as his protective shield. But we feel only tragic sympathy for Hamlet for choosing such a subtle method.

Prof. Nicoll is one of those critics who agrees that Hamlet is really mad, if not throughout, at least at particular moments. Hamlet's bad dreams, restlessness, imperfect sleep, unusual hysterical excitement at particular moments, are specified as vital evidences of his madness. Prof. Nicoll gives seven such instances when Hamlet is insane—the cellarage scene soon after the encounter with the ghost, Hamlet's visit to Ophelia in her closet, the Hecuba soliloquy, the nunnery scene, the end of the Gonzago play, the interview in the Queen's closet, and the grappling in the grave with Laertes.

However, the view that Hamlet is not really mad but feigns madness seems more plausible. At the beginning, as an adolescent, he led a joyful life without any distress. But the world for him is not perfect and wondrous any more. He starts suspecting everything around him including his own actions and emotions; his affection for his mother and uncle; his love for Ophelia; and his friendship. What trouble him most are the injustice, conspiracy, and the betrayal in the society. His father is murdered by his uncle and his mother marries the uncle soon after his father's death. The marriage of his mother is the first blow to him as he had regarded her as a virtuous woman. Then his friends Rosencrantz and Guildenstern are dispatched by the King to spy on him. This is a second blow. Then his girlfriend Ophelia is sent as an agent to find out whether or not he is really mad. One incident after another seems to reveal to him that the time is "out of joint."

Hamlet now becomes aware that he has no access to pursue his ideal and dream. All the glory and the brilliance once he possessed has vanished all of a sudden into the air. The people around him turn to be ignoble and inhuman, and there is no room for reality therefore his life turns out tedious. He wavers in the conflict between the ideal and reality, on the brink of the question—"To be or not to be." All the inequalities and contrast lead him to feigning madness. Life teases him and his madness teases his rivals. Hamlet feels as if he was fooled and the faith he had kept for more than twenty years is shattered by a series of incidents. Therefore, ideal and faith of humanism collapses in his heart. Under such circumstances, Hamlet has no choice but to pretend madness to fight against the foe. He chooses to feign madness which is a need as well as a defence mechanism for him to struggle against reality.

Pretended madness was a widely-used device in the revenge tragedies of Shakespeare's time. "I am but mad north-north west: when the wind is southerly I know a hawk from a handsaw," says Hamlet to Rosencrantz and Guildenstern at the conclusion of their attempts to find out what was wrong with him. Ophelia exclaims, "O, what a noble mind is here overthrown!" after Hamlet verbally abuses her. But the King says: "What he spake, though it lack'd form a little, was not like madness." Further, Polonius says to the King and Queen, "your noble son is mad; mad I call it, for, to define true madness, what is't but to be nothing else but mad?" These remarks by the characters in the play substantiate the view that Hamlet feigns madness.

T. S. Eliot is of the view that "Hamlet's madness is less than madness and more than feigned" (65). According to Eliot, Hamlet's insanity is less than madness for he is never completely out of his senses. He may be thrown off his balance momentarily, but he soon regains self-control. But it is more than feigned, for there are particular scenes in which Hamlet betrays almost delirious excitement and does act as if he were really mad. The modern psychological interpretation agrees with this view. According to the psychologists, there is something morbid and unhealthy about Hamlet's thought process and he is conscious of this. Therefore his assumption of madness is a defence mechanism.

Hamlet pretends to be mad in order to protect himself from the approach of real madness. Insanity often follows when violent emotions are repressed. Hamlet's feignea madness enables him to give free expression to his feelings. It relieves the pressure on his mind and thus saves him from real insanity. It is a psychological necessity. It is more than feigned but less than real. Under the great pressure of multiple contradictions, Hamlet chooses a wise way of becoming mad but seemingly also an undignified one. Having experienced so much struggling, the traces of hatred inside Hamlet have been defeated by his will-power of revenge. Spontaneously, his soul has sublimated to a superior level.

Clearly, Hamlet's insanity is feigned and that he is not really mad at any moment in the play. He himself tells Horatio and Marcellus that he intends to put on an "antic disposition." Moreover, there are definite reasons for his feigned madness. Dowden rightly points out: "He assumes madness as means of concealing his actual disturbance of mind. His over-excitability may betray him: but it be a received opinion that his mind is unhinged, such an excess of over-excitement will pass unobserved and unstudied" (125).

In order to protect himself from the attack of his foes and obtain some intelligence, Hamlet feigns madness. He clearly realises that the world now is extremely dark and unjust and he is bereft of ideas to solve these troubles and eliminate all the devils. The power of his foes he is faced with is so strong that it is impossible for Hamlet to annihilate it on his own and he has to adopt the accessible strategy of pretending lunacy. Hamlet's hesitation of life and death is spelled out in this soliloquy:

> To be, or not to be: that is the question:
> Whether 'tis nobler in the mind to suffer
> The slings and arrows of outrageous fortune,

> Or to take arms against a sea of troubles,
> And by opposing end them? To die; to sleep;
> No more. (3.1.56-61)

This is Hamlet's contemplation of life and death. "To be" means continuing to suffer a lot, "no to be" does not really mean ending all the pains in his heart. Essentially, there lies the cause of his hesitation. And what he can do is just fight a fierce battle that would make him express in angry words, on the one hand, to embody his dissatisfaction and indignation, on the other hand, to protect himself. Naturally his mad words are gifted with a profound allusion to explain his increasing pain of revenge. The significance of his mad words is an insight and dissection of the world as well as an expression of the truth. Beneath his painted madness, Hamlet abandons his dignity, buries his majesty, confronted with loneliness alone. Thus, he decides to wear the mask of madness to severe his connection with the real world. The disguise of madness is the external expression of his hesitation, while his hesitation is the absolute result of his madness. Wilson Knight observes:

> The disguise which he had adopted was not really chosen. The subtlety of his intellect directed him to that tone of wayward sarcasm in which, while he appeared to others to be merely wandering, the bitterness of his soul might be relieved by the utterance of wild and hurling words. But even in this disguise his intellectual supremacy is constantly manifested. (78)

That is why Polonius remarks, "Though this be madness, yet there is method in it." In psychological terms, his madness is significant defence machinery, besides having many other practical advantages. Deighton states, "In every single instance in which Hamlet's madness is manifested, he has good reasons for assuming that madness: while on the one hand, whenever there was no need to hoodwink anyone, his thought, language and action, bear no resemblances of unsoundness of intellect" (205).

Hamlet is mad only with those he wanted to deceive; he is never mad with Horatio or alone by himself. He talks rationally and shows great intellectual power in conversation with Horatio.

Deighton points out: "When he is alone, we have the truth of him, but it is his madness which is on public exhibition" (127). Outside, he is mad; yet inside him, he is clearer than any other.

Psychologists point out that madness causes intense nervous excitement and agitation. After encounter with the ghost, during his visit to Ophelia's closet, and in the graveyard scene, Hamlet certainly loses control over himself and is violently agitated. However, if by sanity we mean that the person concerned is not responsible for his actions, then Hamlet is certainly not mad. At no time can he be regarded as irresponsible. Bradley goes to the root of the matter and points out that Hamlet is not mad. He is fully responsible for his actions, but he suffers from melancholia, a pathological state which may develop into lunacy. His disgust with life can easily assume the form of an irresistible urge for self-destruction. His feelings and will are already disordered and the disorder might easily extend to sense and intellect.

Not only that Shakespeare has concentrated on the feigned madness of Hamlet but also contrasted it with the real madness of Ophelia. Her madness is a case of total insanity resulting from the shock which her tender, innocent nature has received, first, as a result of the horrible murder of her father and secondly from the belief that her rejection of his love has driven to madness of her princely lover. She is a pathetic figure who throws into sharp reflection of the pretended madness of the prince. It is as if Shakespeare wanted to place side by side real with assumed madness.

Hamlet has such a variety of merits as strength, honesty and courage. Admittedly, he is a persistent revenger. And his endurance of humiliation astonishes and moves deeply. He disguises the fire of revenge through the physical madness which makes a striking contrast between him and other avengers who lose and sink in the sea of hatred and revenge. Decisively, Hamlet is not a mad man, but, in contrast, he is a fighter of great courage, a filial son and a laudable prince.

Works Cited

Bradley, A. C. *Shakespearean Tragedy*. Rpt. Calcutta: Reader Publishing, 1988.

Dowden. *Shakespeare's Mind and Art*. New York: Farrar & Rinehart, 1927.

Eliot. T. S. *Hamlet and His Problems*. New Jersey: Prentice Hall, 1968.

Knight, Wilson. *The Crown of Life*. New York: Norton & Co., 1963.

Nicoll, Allardyce. *Shakespeare Survey*. New York: Bantam Books, 1961.

Shakespeare, William. *Hamlet*. New York: Norton & Co., 1963.

19

Hamlet as Defender of Tradition

— S. Bharathiraja

Hamlet the play and Hamlet the character have always attracted the attention of critics with a strong moral bent. This is inevitable because the play deals with crime and its punishment, with complex questions of right and wrong, moral decisions, and moral responsibility for actions. Most of the moral issues raised in *Hamlet* arise from the role imposed on its central character: the role of a revenger.

To appreciate the full implications of these issues, we have to wind back to Elizabethan culture. Shakespeare presents his characters against an obviously Christian background, a background much more distinctively Christian than that of any of his other tragedies. The outlook of the characters has been conditioned by Christian teaching, and the play itself is based on an acceptance of the Catholic teaching on the after-life. The Ghost returning from Purgatory is an example.

This article studies *Hamlet* in the background of such moral issues. It attempts to answer the questions: What are the implications of honour, loyalty, after-life, and revenge in the Elizabethan culture as presented in Shakespeare's play *Hamlet*? How do these implications resonate in modern times? Elizabethan attitudes towards death, suicide, revenge and honour are discussed.

When we first meet Hamlet in Act 1 Scene 2, we see him in a state of despair. He is alone. He talks to himself. He talks about losing interest in life and how upset he is by his mother's remarriage and its implications. (In Shakespeare's era, it was considered morally wrong to marry one's brother's widow.)

Hamlet is trapped in a situation where things are obviously very wrong. Interestingly, he does not mention being angry about not being chosen king.

> *Hamlet*: O that this too too sullied flesh would melt,
> Thaw and resolve itself into a dew,
> Or that the Everlasting had not fix'd
> His canon 'gainst self-slaughter. O God! God!
> How weary, stale, flat, and unprofitable
> Seem to me all the uses of this world!
> Fie on't, ah fie, 'tis an unweeded garden
> That grows to seed; things rank and gross in nature
> Possess it merely. (1.2.129-146)

He longs for death, and would take his own life if suicide were not forbidden by divine decree. The Ghost's response indicates that the doings of a corrupt mortal world are integrated within an eternal world. What Gertrude has done will be taken care of: "Leave her to heaven." But Claudius for his crime is not to be permitted to continue among men and enjoy his booty of crown and queen: "Bear it not." What is unendurable to heaven is not to be endured by men. Evil is not ineradicable, and heaven has appointed an agent of its justice to pluck it out who is Hamlet. He ostentatiously wipes away all previous values, and dedicates himself as a new man.

In Act 3 Scene 1 Hamlet's famous speech on whether it's worthwhile living or doing anything needs little comment. He says it seems to him that life is not worth living, mostly because people treat each other so stupidly and badly. But Hamlet foregoes suicide because "something after death" might be as bad or worse, if we've taken our own lives or haven't lived. He's saying what many people have felt, especially those who do not assume that the Christian account of the afterlife is true — or even that there is any afterlife. Hamlet indeed says that nobody has returned to tell of the afterlife — the ghost notwithstanding. Shakespeare seems to be saying, loud and clear, "Don't focus on the story. Focus on the ideas."

> *Hamlet*: To be, or not to be: that is the question:
> Whether 'tis nobler in the mind to suffer
> The slings and arrows of outrageous fortune,

Or to take arms against a sea of troubles,
And by opposing end them? To die: to sleep;
No more; and by a sleep to say we end
The heart-ache and the thousand natural shocks
That flesh is heir to, 'tis a consummation
Devoutly to be wished. (3.1.56-64)

In Act 5 Scene 1 when two men are digging Ophelia's grave, one asks whether someone who tries to go to heaven by the short route (suicide) can be given Christian burial. In Shakespeare's time, as Hamlet already mentioned in Act 1 Scene 2, suicide was considered a sin, and sometimes even unforgivable. Victims of suicide would ordinarily be buried in unconsecrated ground without a Christian service. Sometimes they would be buried at crossroads (as a warning to everybody not to do the same), and sometimes with a stake through the heart (to prevent them from rising as undead). Similarly, the ghost of Old Hamlet's soul is still roaming.

Hamlet, finding Claudius praying, has a perfect opportunity to kill him, but he does not kill him. He reasons out:

Hamlet: Now might I do it pat, now he is praying.
And now I'll do't. And so he goes to heaven;
And so am I reveng'd. That would be scann'd:
A villain kills my father, and for that,
I, his sole son, do this same villain send
To heaven.
O, this is hire and salary, not revenge. (3.3.72-79)

It is possible to explain these difficulties and the moral confusion surrounding the revenge theme by reminding ourselves that Shakespeare's contemporaries seemed able to accommodate both Christian and pagan ideas of revenge side by side and find justification for each. The world of Hamlet, then, is a Christian one, and the characters view themselves and the significance of their actions and beliefs against Christian teachings and practices. Hamlet embodies two incompatible moral systems, one Christian, the other pagan. Ophelia is in accordance with prescribed Christian ritual in relation to a woman in her circumstances. Claudius at prayer clearly believes in traditional Christian teaching on sin and repentance: without atoning for his crimes, he knows that he cannot earn forgiveness.

By the sixteenth century, with the widespread adoption of the printing press and the increase in the urban population, together with other social changes, the number of fencing treatises being produced increased dramatically. After around 1,500 it seems to have become more socially and legally acceptable to carry swords openly in most parts of Europe, and the increasing fortunes of the middle classes meant that more men were aspiring to carry swords, learn fencing and be seen as gentlemen.

In Act 5 Scene 2, as the king expected, Hamlet is not at all suspicious about the swords, and merely asks whether they are all the same length. In the first round, Hamlet tags Laertes, who is thinking about the poison and perhaps doesn't have his heart really in it. The king drops the poison in the cup, pretending he thinks it's a pearl. Whether the court thinks the pearl is to be dissolved in acidified wine and drunk, or is a gift to Hamlet, you'll need to decide for yourself. The king probably takes a drink (from another cup, or he drinks before the poison is dissolved, or he just pretends to drink. The queen mentions that Hamlet is "fat and out of breath." Fat just means "sweating," so she wipes his forehead. In the second round, Hamlet hits Laertes again. The queen grabs the cup and drinks despite the king's warning. We'll never know whether she has just realized what is going on, and wants to save Hamlet's life and maybe end her own miserable existence:

> *Queen*: No, no, the drink, the drink! O my dear Hamlet,—
> The drink, the drink! I am poison'd. [She Dies] (5.2.315-316)

Laertes tells everything, and shouts "The king's to blame!" For the first time, Hamlet can kill the king and have people realize he was right. Hamlet stabs the king with the poisoned blade, and then forces the poisoned beverage down his throat.

> *King*: O yet defend me, friends. I am but hurt.
> *Hamlet*: Here, thou incestuous, murd'rous, damned Dane,
> Drink off this potion. Is thy union here?
> Follow my mother. [King dies] (5.2.336-338)

> *Laertes*: He is justly serv'd.
> It is a poison temper'd by himself.
> Exchange forgivness with me, noble Hamlet. [Dies]
> (5.2.339-341)

Elizabethans pretended to believe that kings were sacred, so Shakespeare had to have everybody shout "Treason", but nobody does anything. Hamlet says he is dying, and Horatio offers to commit suicide like a Roman soldier when his side was defeated. Hamlet drinks the poison instead, to ensure Horatio won't. If Hamlet saw no reason to live, then Horatio has one—to tell the truth about Hamlet.

> *Hamlet*: Heaven make the free of it. I follow thee.
> I am dead, Horatio. Wretched queen, adieu!
> You that look pale and tremble at this chance,
> That are but mutes or audience to this act,
> Had I but time—as this fell sergeant, Death,
> Is strict in his arrest—O, I could tell you—
> But let it be. Horatio, I am dead,
> Thou livest. Report me and my cause aright
> To the unsatisfied. (5.2.342-350)

Horatio says he'll tell about "accidental judgments", which is the theme of God working in the world to make things right.

> *Horatio*: Now cracks a noble heart. Good night, sweet prince,
> And flight of angels sing thee to thy rest. (5.2.364-365)

Fortinbras calls for military honours to be shown to Hamlet's body. Some people see this recovery of ceremonial to mean things are right with the world again. Others will simply see one more example of power passing in an unfair world—as it was in the real Dark Ages.

> *Fortinbras*: Let four captains
> Bear Hamlet like a soldier to the stage,
> For he was likely, had he been put on,
> To have prov'd most royal; and for his passage,
> The soldier's music and the rite of war
> Speak loudly for him. (5.2.400-409)

Hamlet is the first work of literature to look squarely at the stupidity, falsity and sham of everyday life, without laughing and without easy answers. In a world where things are not as they seem, Hamlet's genuineness, thoughtfulness, and sincerity make him special.

Hamlet reaffirms the tragic dignity of a basically decent person in a bad world. *Hamlet* is the first work of literature to show an ordinary person looking at the futility and wrongs in life, asking the toughest questions and coming up with honest answers. Unlike so much of popular culture today, *Hamlet* leaves us with the message that life is indeed worth living, even by imperfect people in an imperfect world. The bound between a language and the culture to which it refers cannot be neglected if we work our students to understand the language fully and to use it proficiently.

Works Cited

Knight, Wilson. *The Wheel of Fire*. New York: Routledge, 2001.

Sofield, Martin. *Hamlet*. Cambridge: CUP, 1980.

Evangelista, Nick. *The Art and Science of Fencing*. Indianapolis: Masters Press, 1996.

"Shakespeare's Hamlet shows Christian hopefuleness at death." 8 th Jan. 2009. <www.bagpipeonline.com>

20

Anti-Semitism in *The Merchant of Venice*

— Colette Sharmila

Anti-Semitism is a term used to describe prejudice against people of Jewish lineage, which is based upon a historical religio-cultural aversion to their core ancestral religious beliefs and way of life. Jews have lived as a religious minority in Christian and Muslim lands. Christianity and Islam have both portrayed Jews as those who rejected God's truth. Jews suffer bigotry and other forms of ill-treatment because of their religion and race. Christians alienate Shylock simply because he is a Jew. In ancient medieval and Renaissance times, Jews almost always encountered prejudice from non-Jews around them.

Prejudice against Jews increased in England around 1190 after non-Jews borrowed heavily from Jewish moneylenders becoming deeply indebted to them. In York, about 150 Jews committed suicide to avoid being captured by an angry mob. Richard I put a stop to Jewish persecution, but it returned in the following century during the reign of Edward I from 1272 to 1307. The state required Jews to wear strips of yellow cloth as identification, taxed them heavily and forbade them to mingle with Christians. Finally in 1290 Edward banished them from England. Only a few Jews remained behind.

Intolerance of Jews was a fact of the sixteenth century life even in Venice, the most powerful and liberal state in Europe. By law the Jews were forced to live in the old walled foundry or ghetto area of the city. After sun-down the gate was locked and guarded by Christians. In the day-time any man leaving the ghetto had to wear a red hat to mark him as a Jew. The Jews were forbidden to own property. So they practised usury, the lending of money at interest. This was against Christian law. The sophisticated Venetians would turn a blind eye to it but for the religious fanatics, who hated the Jews, it was another matter.

During the Elizabethan period, anti-Semitism remained in force. Christopher Marlowe, a contemporary of Shakespeare, wrote a play entitled, *The Jew of Malta,* which depicted a Jew named Barabas as a savage murderer:

> "Rather had I, a Jew: be hated thus,
> Than pities in a Christian poverty
> For I can see no fruits in all their faith,
> But malice, falsehood, and excessive pride,
> Which methinks fits not their prince. (1.117-121)

The above extract from *The Jew of Malta* obviously pictures the nature of anti-Semitism that was prevalent in England. In *The Jew of Malta* the title character, Barabas is detested to that extent that his enemies boil him in a cauldron. Audience loved the play, many of them not realizing that Marlowe's main intent was to satirize Christians, and it probably influenced Shakespeare in his depiction of Shylock.

In *The Merchant of Venice* Shakespeare acknowledges the existence of prejudice, and makes use of it to suit his dramatic ends. The topics that the play presents include social hatred, colour prejudice, class distinction and the position of women in society. In this play the term racism denotes violence against Shylock and how this character is oppressed by the so called inherent superior Christian race. Shylock, the money-lender who is hated because he is a Jew, explains how prejudice works: "Affection/Master of passion, sways it to the mood of what it likes and/Loathes" (4.1.50-52).

Shylock starts from a double disadvantage, as far as an Elizabethan audience was concerned. He is a Jew and he is a money-lender. Shylock first appears as the cautious businessman, thinking carefully before he invests his three thousand ducats in Bassania's enterprise. To some extent Shylock justifies his hostility when he describes how he has been treated by Antonio:

> Signor Antonio, many a time and often
> In the rialto you have rated me
> About my moneys and my usances
> Still have I borne it with a patient shrug,
> For sufferance is the badge of all our tribe
> You call me misbeliever, cut throat dog,
> And spit upon my Jewish gabardine,
> And all for use of that which is mine own.
> Well then, it now appears you need. (1.3.102-110)

Shylock retaliates when Antonio approaches Shylock for three thousand ducats: "Hath a dog money? Is it possible/A cur can lend three thousand ducats?" (1.3.117-118). One can understand that the sarcasm the Christians have taught Shylock is used by Shylock. Shylock's passion is subdued into an intense and malevolent bitterness, when one comes across the fisting of the two Christians is cruel. The loss of a daughter earns pity in this scene. Solanio instead of consoling Shylock enjoys the way Shylock lar ents over her daughter's elopement:

> I never heard a passion so confus'd.
> So strange, outrageous, and so variable,
> As the dog Jew did utter in the streets:
> 'my daughter! O my ducats! O my daughter!' 2.8.12-15)

Solanio ridicules Shylock's outburst of feeling after Jessica's elopement. It is with very mixed feelings, then, that we are led up to speech in which Shylock catalogues the abuses he has had to suffer from Christians in general, and from Antonio in particular. There is only one reason that he can see for this treatment: "I am a Jew." It is easy to respond to the rhetorical questions that follow:

> Hath not a Jew eyes? Hath not a Jew hands, organs, dimensions, senses, affections, passions? Fed with the same food, hurt with the same weapons, subject to the same diseases, healed by the same means, warmed and cooled by the same winter and summer, as a Christian is? If you prick us, do we not bleed? If you tickle us, do we not laugh? If you poison us, do we not die? (3.1.54—62)

Shylock appeals to our humanity. To give a negative answer to his questions would deny not his humanity, but our own. "The villainy you teach me I will execute, and it shall go hard but will better the instruction" (3.1.67-69). Shylock will "better the instruction", and prove himself to be not the equal of the Christians in inflicting suffering on others, but their superior.

During the trial, Shylock demands a strict observance of the law, and (in poetic justice) it is precisely this that defeats him. Gratiano gets wild when Shylock makes a wolfish demand of taking a pound of flesh from Antonio:

> And whilst thou lay'st in thy
> unhallow'd elam, infus'd itself
> in thee; for thy desires are
> wolvish, bloody, starv'd and ravenous. (4.1.136-138)

One can make out that Gratiano goes to the extent of abusing Shylock's mother's womb. The cruel mind of Gratiano reflects that racial discrimination dominates the mind of every Christian in Venice. Christian hypocrisy is never more odious, though, than during the trial. First the duke asks Shylock, ready to claim his pound of flesh, "How shalt thou hope for mercy, rendering none?" (4.1.92). Ever outspoken Shylock replies: "what judgment shall I dread, doing no wrong?" (4.1.93)

Then, after Portia speaks eloquently of the need of clemency and compassion in her 'quality of mercy' courtroom speech, she and her friends humiliate Shylock. Shylock is eased out of his money by the verbal pyro-techniques of Portia. And he is also forced to accept Christianity. After the trial, without the slightest prick of conscience, the Christians hie off to Belmont—a kind of way station between this world and heaven—to partake in the pleasures of the idle highborn and wealthy. They have their pound of flesh, Shylock's heart. They also have his daughter, a convert to Christianity.

In the end, Shylock, becomes a victim of a perverse world, a victim of people who mislead, misuse and prejudge him—and force him to take a desperate stand and lose everything. The Christians, meanwhile live happily ever after, allowing the play to be called a comedy. But it is not a true comedy. At the end, while Christians exult in their victory at Belmont, one can imagine Shylock walking the streets of the Rialto or the Jewish Ghetto looking for his dignity and the glow of a friendly candle.

Works Cited

Marlowe, Christopher. *The Jew of Malta* in *The Plays of Christopher Marlowe*. London: OUP, 1939.

Amoko, Apollo. "Race and Post Coloniality." *The Routledge Companion to Critical Theory*. Ed. Simon Malpas and Paul Wake. New York: Routledge, 2006.

Shakespeare, William. *The Merchant of Venice*. Ed. John Russell Brown. New Delhi: Methuen & Co. Ltd, 2008.

21

Pericles and the Sea: An Archetypal Reading of *Pericles: Prince of Tyre*

— Suresh Frederick

Archetype means chief type or a primordial shaping influence. This is the most primitive, because it goes deep into the vicissitudes of primordial influence of myth; and it is also modern. It comes with much force because it introduces the unconscious. Thus, archetypes are visual symbols or energetic imprints that exist in our psyche. Some are readily understood while others bring subliminal messages that are there to help us trigger our memory of why we are here and the truth behind the illusion of reality. Archetypes can often convey messages that verbal and written information cannot.

Archetypes are found everywhere, as their symbols are a language of the mind, taken to different frequencies of thought and connected to each other by the collective unconscious. At times, it comes as a kind of epiphanic revelation as it influences religion. Social customs too are related to myth. Thus archetypes emerge through centuries, crossing regional and national boundaries. Hence they can be categorised as both individual and universal.

There are individual and universal archetypes. The term archetype gained popularity with Carl Jung. In Jung's terms, "Archetype" is defined as the first original model of which all other similar persons, objects, or concepts are merely derivative, copied, patterned or emulated. Archetypes are innate prototypes for ideas, which may subsequently become involved in the interpretation of observed phenomena. Jung opines that archetypes are important to an extent that its retention, if articulated, is the best experience in literature. If Jung calls it "collective unconscious," Eliot calls it "European Consciousness."

Archetypal literary criticism is a type of critical theory that interprets a text by focusing on recurring myths and archetypes (from the Greek *archç*, or beginning; and *typos*, or imprint) in the narratives, symbols, images, and character types in a literary work. As a form of literary criticism, it dates back to 1934 when Maud Bodkin published *Archetypal Patterns in Poetry*. Its origins are rooted in two other academic disciplines, social anthropology and psychoanalysis; each contributed to the literary criticism in distinct ways, with the latter being a sub-branch of literary critical theory. Archetypal criticism was very popular in the 1950's and 1960's, largely due to the work of the Canadian literary critic Northrop Frye. Frye was greatly inspired by the patterns of myth. T.S. Eliot's use of many myths in *The Wasteland,* for instance, serves as a unifying factor bringing the past and the present ever close together. James Frazer's and Jung's contribution is immensely appreciated in this context. Archetypes are the central unifying factor in any text.

Herman Northrop Frye (1912-1991), a Canadian, was one of the most distinguished literary critics and literary theorists of the twentieth century. Frye gained international fame with his first book, *Fearful Symmetry* (1947), which led to the reinterpretation of the poetry of William Blake. His lasting reputation rests principally on the theory of literary criticism that he developed in *Anatomy of Criticism* (1959), one of the leading works of literary theory published in the twentieth century. Frye's contributions to cultural and social criticism spanned a long career during which he earned widespread recognition and received many honours.

Northrop Frye talks about the sea as an archetype in *The Archetypes of Literature*. The sea has become a very important archetype in literature. No writer can say that the sea image belongs to him or her. It is an archetype of literature. With Auden's essay, "The Enchafed Flood" as a reference, Frye writes, " . . . an important symbol like the sea cannot remain within the poetry of Shelley or Keats or Coleridge; it is bound to expand over many poets into an archetypal symbol of literature" (Lodge 426).

Frye presents two visions, namely, the comic vision and the tragic vision. He speaks of five worlds, namely, the human world, the animal world, the vegetable world, the mineral world and the unformed world (Lodge 432). He classifies the sea under the unformed world that comes with the broadly classified tragic vision. "In tragic vision the world usually becomes the sea. . . . The combination of the sea and beast images gives us the leviathan and similar sea-monsters" (Lodge 432).

Pericles, Prince of Tyre, probably written in 1607-8, came late in Shakespeare's career, after some of his most powerful dramas, such as *Hamlet, Macbeth, King Lear,* and *Othello.* Yet, this play is far more different than those grand plays. James F. Bellman and Kathryn Bellman say, "This play was popular in Shakespeare's time, but since then, it has fallen into relative obscurity" (quoted in Carey 301). This play tells the story of Pericles, the young prince of Tyre in Phoenicia (now Lebanon). Hoeniger comments, "One can infer from Pericles' talents and activities that he is a man of unusual gifts, a skilful soldier as well as a great musician, a man of great authority among his subjects, and of generous dealing"(lxxx). The other important characters in the play are Thaisa, daughter of Simonides and Marina, daughter of Pericles and Thaisa.

This paper tries to consider the sea as an archetype and also to analyze its significance as a backdrop to the play. In *Pericles,* the title-hero, Pericles, encounters the sea and a sea storm. The play opens in the court of Antiochus, King of Antioch, who will offer the hand of his beautiful daughter to any man who answers his riddle; but those who fail shall die:

> I am no viper, yet I feed
> On mother's flesh which did me breed.
> I sought a husband, in which labour
> I found that kindness in a father:
> He's father, son, and husband mild;
> I mother, wife, and yet his child.
> How they may be, and yet in two,
> As you will live, resolve it you. (1.1. 65-72)

Pericles, the young Prince of Tyre, correctly guesses that the daughter of Antiochus is involved in an incestuous affair with her father. Antiochus knows that Pericles knows, and Pericles knows it. His life is in danger. Pericles wisely flees Antioch for Tyre.

Antiochus intends to kill him, however; Pericles appoints his counsellor Helicanus to rule as regent and then sails from Tyre for Tarsus, then Pentapolis.

In Tarsus, the citizens are suffering a great famine. When Pericles arrives, the Lord Governor Cleon wonders whether the royal visitor means to take advantage of the situation and make war. But Pericles tells Cleon that he has come in peace with a shipload of corn, for he has heard of the starvation in Tarsus and means to distribute the corn to the people. After Cleon comes to know of the good intentions of Pericles, he heartily welcomes Pericles, the prince's men unload the corn, and Tarsus is saved. Here, for Tarsus, the saviour has come through the sea.

While sailing home, Pericles encounters a terrible storm and is shipwrecked, so informs Gower in the dumb show preceding Act 2:

> He, doing so, put forth to seas,
> Where when men been, there's seldom ease;
> For now the wind begins to blow;
> Thunder above and deeps below
> Make such unquiet, that the ship
> Should house him safe is wreck'd and split; (27-32)

The sea plays a vital role here. The strong winds have broken Pericles' ship. He has become an insignificant person with no servants and no wealth to support him. He is the lonely survivor:

> And he, good prince, having all lost,
> By waves from coast to coast is tost:
> All perishen of man, of pelf,
> Ne aught escapen but himself;
> Till fortune, tired with doing bad,
> Threw him ashore, to give him glad: (33-38)

Thus, the vessel is shipwrecked, and Pericles is the sole survivor. Pericles enters the stage completely wet in Act 2 Scene 1 and says:

> Yet cease your ire, you angry stars of heaven!
> Wind, rain, and thunder, remember, earthly man
> Is but a substance that must yield to you; (2. 1. 1-3)

Pericles pleads with nature to stop the fury. He acknowledges that human beings have to obey this "angry star of heavens":

> And I, as fits my nature, do obey you:
> Alas, the sea hath cast me on the rocks,
> Wash'd me from shore to shore, and left me breath
> Nothing to think on but ensuing death:
> Let it suffice the greatness of your powers
> To have bereft a prince of all his fortunes;
> And having thrown him from your watery grave,
> Here to have death in peace is all he'll crave. (2. 1. 4-11)

He is ready to live with nature without complaining about the ferocity let loose by it. He loses all his fortunes, but the sea helps him come out of the "watery grave." He clambers onshore and speaks of his misfortune. Then fishermen and their master help him to recover.

At Pentapolis, Pericles participates in a tournament for the hand of Thaisa, daughter of Simonides. He wins the tournament and Pericles marries Thaisa. In the meantime, news arrives that Antiochus is dead and that the people of Tyre want their prince back. Pericles makes arrangements to sail for Tyre with Thaisa, who is now pregnant with their child. On Pericles's sea voyage back to Tyre with Thaisa, thunder booms and lightning flashes, just as Thaisa goes into labour. A storm along the way brings about the birth of Marina, their daughter; Thaisa, tragically, is believed to have died in childbirth. Charles Lamb writes, "The sea was no friendly element to unhappy Pericles, for long before they reached Tyre, another dreadful tempest arose, which so terrified Thaisa that she was taken ill, and in a short space of time her nurse Lychorida came to Pericles with a little child in her arms, to tell the prince the sad tidings that his wife died the moment her little babe was born" (http://shakespeare.palomar.edu). Pericles cries in agony:

> O, still
> Thy deafening, dreadful thunders; gently quench
> Thy nimble, sulphurous flashes! O, how, Lychordia,
> How does my queen? Thou stormest venomously;
> Wilt thou spit all thyself? (3. 1. 4-8)

Here also the sea plays a role in wrecking the family of Pericles. Storm, thunder and lightning have made a dent in the life of Pericles.

When Thaisa dies, the ship's sailors wish to have her body removed immediately from the ship, believing that the storm battering them will not cease until the ship be cleared of the dead body. Sailors felt that proper burial rituals are absolutely essential to prevent haunting. They feared disposing of a body without a formal ceremony. Benjamin Sell in "Burial at Sea and Shakespeare's *Pericles*" writes, "The sailors on Pericles' ship feared the bad luck Thaisa's spirit could bring, and as such wanted her body off the ship and beyond the barrier of the water's surface as soon as possible" (http://shakespeareantheatre.suite101.com). Pericles is very sad. He says:

> A terrible childbed hast thou had, my dear;
> No light, no fire: the unfriendly elements
> Forgot thee utterly; nor have I time
> To give thee hallow'd to thy grave, but straight
> Must cast thee, scarcely coffin'd, in the ooze;
> Where, for a monument upon thy bones,
> And e'er-remaining lamps, the belching whale
> And humming water must o'erwhelm thy corpse,
> Lying with simple shells. O Lychorida,
> Bid Nestor bring me spices, ink and paper,
> My casket and my jewels; and bid Nicander
> Bring me the satin coffer: lay the babe
> Upon the pillow: hie thee, whiles I say
> A priestly farewell to her: suddenly, woman.(3. 1. 56-69)

Sealing her in a watertight coffin, Pericles gives her a burial at sea. The coffin washes up on the shores of Ephesus, where Cerimon manages to revive Thaisa. Unsurprisingly, Thaisa assumes that Pericles is lost at sea and promptly becomes a votaress in the Temple of Diana.

On the way back to Tyre, Pericles leaves Marina at Tarsus for Cleon and his wife to bring her up. He says:

> We cannot but obey
> The powers above us. Could I rage and roar

As doth the sea she lies in, yet the end
Must be as 'tis. My gentle babe, Marina, whom,
For she was born at sea, I have named so, here
I charge your charity withal, leaving her
The infant of your care; beseeching you
To give her princely training, that she may be
Manner'd as she is born. (3. 3. 9-17)

Pericles sails on for Tyre. Fast forward sixteen years, when she is there, her speech is overloaded with reference to the sea. Marina says:

No, I will rob Tellus of her weed,
To strew thy green with flowers: the yellows, blues,
The purple violets, and marigolds,
Shall as a carpet hang upon thy grave,
While summer-days do last. Ay me! poor maid,
Born in a tempest, when my mother died,
This world to me is like a lasting storm,
Whirring me from my friends. (4. 1. 13-20)

But, this beautiful Marina has stirred the jealousy of Dionyza, who resolves to have her murdered. Dionyza's servant, who is entrusted with the job, cannot carry it out because Marina is captured by pirates; the servant reports back that Marina is dead, and Cleon mournfully raises a monument to her memory. Pericles encounters the tomb on a visit to Tarsus and falls into a deep despair. The pirates, meanwhile, sell Marina into a brothel in Mitylene, but she is soon freed by the governor.

Pericles sails into Mitylene still deeply depressed about the supposed loss of his daughter. While there, he comes upon Marina, and after some talking, Pericles eventually recognizes her for his daughter; the two are happily reunited. Lysismachus, the governor, asks for Marina's hand, which Marina accepts. Then, Pericles is visited by a dream that instructs him to visit Ephesus. Then he goes to Ephesus. There he says to the chief votaress of Goddess Diana:

Hail, Diana! to perform thy just command,
I here confess myself the king of Tyre;
Who, frighted from my country, did wed

At Pentapolis the fair Thaisa.
At sea in childbed died she, but brought forth
A maid-child call'd Marina; who, O goddess,
Wears yet thy silver livery. She at Tarsus
Was nursed with Cleon; who at fourteen years
He sought to murder: but her better stars
Brought her to Mytilene; 'gainst whose shore
Riding, her fortunes brought the maid aboard us,
Where, by her own most clear remembrance, she
Made known herself my daughter. (5. 3 1-13)

There he is reunited as well with Thaisa who is now the votaress of Diana, and the whole family is together again.

The simplicity of relationships, the unlikelihood of the events and the lack of cause and effect in the plot, make the play a representation of images which, while individually they expand into wide and general meanings, yet as part of a sequence, they withdraw from asserting how things run in this world. The reader is offered ideas or propositions about love and suffering and chastity, and the relation of them to the divine will, but no one is offered a clue to any meaning lying in the progression of events. The sea, therefore, remains a mystery. Neptune and Aeolus, the waves and the wind, are great forces and the lives of human beings are in their hands. There is a suggestion of divine control but no one can understand its pattern. The terrible power of the sea has helped the fulfilment of the great triangle of affection represented by Pericles, Thaisa, and Marina.

Neptune is the divinity that makes the strongest appearance in Pericles. Neptune is the sea god, to whom Pericles appeals in the storm as "The god of this great vast." The last mention of Neptune in the play is important. The reunion between Marina and Pericles takes place in Pericles' ship in the harbour at Mytilene, where, the "annual feast" of "god Neptune" is being celebrated by the town. The feast is mentioned a second time by Lysimachus (5. 1. 16). It seems that a point is being made when father and daughter are brought together in the harbour, where, after so many storms, the sea is quiet, in a city where the annual feast of the sea god is being celebrated.

Thus the backdrop for the whole story is the sea. According

to Frye's classification, throughout the play, the sea is an archetype under "the tragic vision" (Lodge 432). The sea, because of its immense power and fury, encompasses "the tragic vision." But it makes amends for the damage done. Even though Pericles calls it the "watery grave" it takes him safely to the shore in spite of the raging tempest which leaves him bereft of all his fortunes. Again, we see that Pericles is in a situation where he is unable to join the birthday celebration of Simonides's daughter where many knights will assemble in a tournament to win her love. And here again, it is the sea which restores his armour to him, through some fishermen. It is Thaisa's death that is considered to be the most tragic event through the course of the play, but in the end it is again the sea which washes her coffin safely on to the shore. The sea brings about calamities, but surely makes necessary amends. F.D.Hoeniger feels that "the storms and shipwrecks" (1xxx) are very significant events in the play. And undoubtedly the play ends in a happy note and thus comes under "the comic vision." Thus the sea, just like the island archetype, becomes a "neutral archetype" (Lodge 433). As Frye says, "It is of course only the general comic or tragic context that determines the interpretation of any symbol. . . ." (Lodge 433). Thus the archetypal image acts as a "hunch" (Lodge 433) to understand the structure of the play.

Works Cited

Carey, Gary. Ed. *Shakespeare's Minor Plays*. Nebraska: Cliffs, 1991.

Edwards, Philip. Ed. *Shakespeare: Pericles, Prince of Tyre*. New York: Penguin, 1981.

Hoeniger, F.D Ed. *Pericles*. London: Methuen, 1969.

Lodge, David. Ed. *Twentieth Century Literary Criticism: A Reader*. New York: Longman, 1972.

Sell, Benjamin. "Burial at Sea and Shakespeare's *Pericles*." <http://shakespeareantheatre.suite101.com/article.cfm/burial_at_sea_and_shakespeares_pericles>

The Contributors

K. Chellappan is an eminent scholar in comparative literature and was the first Faculty Head of Department of English, Bharathidasan University, Tiruchy. He has also served as Director of State Institute of English, Tamil Nadu, Chennai and has to his credit critical works on Indian and European literatures. He has also published on ancient and modern Tamil literature.

B. Hariharan teaches at the Institute of English, University of Kerala, Thiruvananthapuram. He worked earlier at the Post Graduate Centre, University of Mysore, Hassan and at Prajyoti Niketan College, Pudukad, and Christ College, Irinjalakuda, Kerala. He has published articles in journals and edited two books, and translated three books from Malayalam to English.

Banibrata Goswami is Assistant Professor of English at Panchakot Mahavidyalaya, Sarbari More, Purulia District, West Bengal since 2003. He specialises in nationalism and postcolonialism. He is also conducting a UGC MRP in the same field. His other interests are Shakespeare, Yeats, Tagore and Vijay Tendulkar. He edits an ISSN journal *Panchakot Essays.*

Raju Parghi is Research Scholar in English at Pondicherry University.

Harini Jayaraman is Chairperson, Department of English, Amrita School of Engineering, Coimbatore; **K. Sreena** is Lecturer in English, Amrita School of Engineering, Coimbatore. She is working for her Ph. D. on film studies.

Punyashree Panda is Assistant Professor of English at Indian Institute of Technology, Bhubaneswar. She has more than 15 conference presentations and several national and international research publications to her credit. Her areas of interest include Native American and Native Canadian Fiction, Postcolonialism, Indian Writing in English, Cross Cultural Communication, and English Language Teaching.

Aysha Viswamohan is Assistant Professor at Indian Institute of Technology, Chennai. Her teaching and research areas include Film Studies, Drama and Communication. She has published four books including *Arthur Miller:The Dramatist and His Universe* (2006) and *English for Technical Communication* (2007-2008). She has over thirty papers on language and literature in Indian as well as international journals, and has presented several papers in international conferences at UK, Singapore and Malaysia. She is on the editorial boards of many internationally referred journals, including *Journal of English for Specific Purposes, Asian EFLJ, Journal of Intercultural Communication* (Sweden) and is a referee for *Modern Language Journal* (Blackwell: USA). She is the Indian representative for the Special Interest Group of IATEFL (UK), and was awarded the Ray Tongue Scholarship (UK).

T. Asha Priya is Senior Lecturer in English, School of Engineering, Amrita Viswa Vidyapeetham, Coimbatore; **M.G. Priya** is Lecturer in English at School of Engineering, Amrita Viswa Vidyapeetham, Coimbatore.

Shruti Bidwaikar is Ph.D. Scholar in English at Pondicherry University. She has done her MA in English from Fergusson College, Pune and is working on Sri Aurobindo's Aesthetics and has published four papers in this area.

T. Deivasigamani is Assistant Professor of English and the Coordinator of SC/ST Special Cell, Annamalai University. He specialises in African American and Dalit Studies. He has presented 16 papers at national and international level; published six articles and one book. He is currently working on a UGC Major Project in Dalit Studis.

Geetha Sentthil Kumar is Assistant Professor (Senior Grade) at School of Engineering, Amrita Viswa Vidyapeetham, Coimbatore. Her area of interest is American Literature. She is a Cambridge University certified trainer for Business English Course. She is Member of Board of Studies in English at Avinashilingam University for Women, Coimbatore; **P. Ambika**

is Senior Lecturer and **K.A. Krishnalalitha** is Lecturer at School of Engineering, Amrita Viswa Vidyapeetham, Coimbatore.

N.Chandra is Ph.D. Scholar in English at Pondicherry University. Her area of research is Masculinities in Post-independent Indian Novels. She has two paper publications and 17 paper presentations at national level seminars.

M. Smitha is Lecturer in English, Amrita School of Engineering, Coimbatore.

S. Subhapriya is Ph.D. Scholar in English at Pondicherry University. Her current area of research is Sports Fiction. She has to her credit five paper presentations at national level seminars.

M. Parimala is Ph.D. Scholar in English at Pondicherry University. Her research interest is Contemporary American Literature. She was awarded the Pre-Doctoral Fellowship for the year 2008-2009 by Osmania University Centre for International Programs (OUCIP), Hyderabad.

V. Sangeetha is Reader in English, Periyar University, Salem. She is interested in Commonwealth Literature, Shakespeare Studies, British Literature and Literary Criticism. She is a life member in many International and National Associations for Literature. She has presented a number of papers in International, National Conferences. Some of her articles are published in leading Literary Journals.

C. Santhosh Kumar is Reader in English, Directorate of Distance Education, Annamalai University. His interests are TESOL and Shakespeare Studies. Shakespeare is his reference, he says, for resolving unanswered questions of life.

K. Ravichandran is Assistant Professor, Department of English, Annamalai University. He has published several articles in journals of national and international repute. He is a recipient of Dr. Ambedkar's Fellowship Award 2008. His areas of interest include Indian Writing in English, Dalit Literature, American literature and Modern Criticism.

S. Bharathiraja is UGC Project Fellow on Dalit Studies, Department of English, Annamalai University. He has presented and published papers on Discourse Analysis and ELT. He is currently working on the exploitation, emancipation and empowerment components in Dalit and Tribal Indian novels.

Colette Sharmila is Assistant Professor of English, V.O.C. College, Tuticorin. Her current area of research is Anglo-Indian Fiction. She has presented three papers in National Seminars and one in an International Seminar. She has three publications in multidisciplinary research journals.

Suresh Frederick is Associate Professor and UG Head, Department of English, Bishop Heber College, Trichy. He has twenty years of teaching experience. He specializes in Ecocriticism, Mass Communication, ELT, Australian Literature, American Literature and British Drama. He has presented many papers in International and National conferences and published many papers in reputed books and journals. He is the Vice President of OSLE (Organization for Study of Literature and Environment) and a Member of the Andrew Marvell Society and an Associate Member of the Council for Research in Values and Philosophy, Washington, D.C.